KNOWING
CHRISTIANITY

J. I. PACKER

InterVarsity Press
Downers Grove, Illinois

InterVarsity Press
P.O. Box 1400, Downers Grove, IL 60515
World Wide Web: www.ivpress.com
E-mail: mail@ivpress.com

InterVarsity Press® *is the book-publishing division of InterVarsity Christian Fellowship/USA*®, *a student movement active on campus at hundreds of universities, colleges and schools of nursing in the United States of America, and a member movement of the International Fellowship of Evangelical Students. For information about local and regional activities, write Public Relations Dept., InterVarsity Christian Fellowship/USA, 6400 Schroeder Rd., P.O. Box 7895, Madison, WI 53707-7895.*

Cover photograph: Zeta-Germany/The Stock Market

ISBN 0-8308-2216-X

Printed in the United States of America ♾

Library of Congress Cataloging-in-Publication Data
Packer, J. I. (James Innell)
    Knowing Christianity/ J.I. Packer
        p.   cm.
    Originally published: Wheaton, Ill.: Harold Shaw Publishers.
    c1995.
    Includes bibliographical references.
    ISBN 0-8308-2216-X (pbk.: alk. paper)
    1. Theology, Doctrinal Popular works.   I. Title.
    [BT77.P237   1999]
    230—dc21   99-29790
                                                                                         CIP

20	19	18	17	16	15	14	13	12	11	10	9	8	7	6	5	4	3	2	1
18	17	16	15	14	13	12	11	08	07	06	05	04	03	02	01	00	99		

To the people of St. John's Anglican Church,
Shaughnessy, Vancouver,
through whom and with whom
I receive so much

CONTENTS

To the Reader

I have never been through a major earthquake, but I would be a fool to assume I never will. I live in Vancouver, Canada, where we are now being told that a big one could happen at any time and that there is almost certain to be a big one sometime in the next two centuries. I have seen pictures, as I am sure you have, of the devastation in Los Angeles, California, and Kobe, Japan, following their big ones, and the thought that Vancouver may suffer the same way is chilling, to say the least.

What can be done about an earthquake threat? Not a lot, really. But Vancouver is doing what it can. New buildings now must comply with an earthquake building code; old buildings and public works are being strengthened to meet the code's requirements; and we have all been directed to fasten bookcases and other collapsibles to the wall, to learn how to switch everything off at the point of supply, and to dive under the table the moment the tremor starts. What we are being told, in Scout language, is that we must *be prepared.*

Wise Christians prepare not only for natural disasters—earthquake, fire, flood—but also for their intellectual, relational and circumstantial counterparts. Christians are not exempt from what Shakespeare called "the slings and arrows of outrageous fortune." Pains and griefs, hurts and humblings come to Christians as to others, and we constantly find ourselves having to swim against the stream at work, at home and even in church. How can we prepare ourselves for such traumas? The best we can do is make sure the foundations of our faith are solid, the specifics of it are firmly anchored in our minds, and our habits of devotion and goodwill are as they should be. If we are Christ's, the devil will constantly be after us; shakings and quakings will come, and Satan will try to use them to unbalance and undermine us. "So put on all the armor that God gives. Then when the evil day comes, you will be able to defend yourself. And when the battle is over, you will still be standing firm" (Eph 6:13 CEV).

The following chapters are offered as a help in preparing for life's earthquakes, especially as they strike at mainstream Christianity. The book centers on fundamentals of faith and action on which, as I see it, all believers need to be very clear and strong at the present time. It addresses ordinary people who mean business with our extraordinary God and his extraordinary Son, our Savior Jesus Christ. It is not a technical work but, in intention at any rate, a plain and practical one (no footnotes, therefore, no academic arguments and no denominational sidetracks). Fifty years ago a popular Christian book was titled *The Iron Ration of a Christian.* That title, I believe, would fit what is set out here.

Thanks are due to Ramona Tucker, Joan Guest, Stephen Board and my daughter Naomi for helping to put *Knowing Christianity* into shape. I have not tried to remove all traces of the oral origin of some of the chapters or the occasional partial repetitions that their arguments involve; life's too short! The book now goes out with the prayer that God will use it to do some good.

1

THE MOST IMPORTANT THING OF ALL

K NOWING GOD. IS THERE ANY GREATER THEME TO STUDY? Is there any nobler goal to aim at? Is there any greater good to enjoy? Is there any deeper longing in the human heart than the desire to know God? Surely not. And Christianity's good news is that it can happen! That is why the Christian message is a word for the world. To know God is the biggest and best of the blessings promised in the gospel. Equally, knowing God is celebrated in the Scriptures as the supreme gift of grace. Jeremiah, looking forward to what God was going to do, spoke in these terms: " 'The time is coming,' declares the LORD, 'when I will make a new covenant with the house of Israel.' " And the consequence will be this: "No longer will a man teach his neighbor, or a man his brother, saying, 'Know the LORD,' because they will all know me, from the least of them to the greatest" (Jer 31:31, 34). The fulfillment of this promise is the glory of Christianity. Christians know God. Everyone may know God.

Jesus Christ came as a preacher of eternal life. On one occasion, in prayer to his Father, he defined eternal life. "Now this is eternal life," he said: "that they may know you, the only true God, and Jesus Christ, whom you have sent" (Jn 17:3). The apostle John, the beloved disciple who leaned on Jesus' breast at the Last Supper and perhaps saw deeper into Jesus' heart of love than anyone else, sums up at the end of his first letter what Christ has brought to him and his fellow believers: "We know also that the Son of God has come and has given us understanding, so that we may know him who is true" (1 Jn 5:20). *True* here means not only truthful and trustworthy as opposed to deceitful and unreliable but also "real" as opposed to imaginary. John is telling us that Christians know—that is, are consciously and cognitively related to—the personal mind and power that is behind everything. And this knowledge is itself a personal relationship, knowledge-in-union and knowledge-in-fellowship, a precious reality of experience for which "eternal life" is the proper name. So he continues: "And we are in him who is true—even in his Son Jesus Christ. He is the true God and eternal life" (v. 20).

Such is the glorious reality of knowing God. For this we were made, and for this we have been redeemed. This is the true object of the world's longing and the sum and substance of the Christian's ambition and hope. The apostle Paul states his own life goal in these terms: "I want to know Christ" (Phil 3:10). The hope to which Paul looks forward he sums up in this way: "Now I know in part; then I shall know fully, even as I am fully known" (1 Cor 13:12). Paul's ambition and his hope are focused in terms of the knowledge of God. As for him, so for us: it is our highest dignity, our proper purpose and our final fulfillment to know God. There is, I repeat, no more vital subject that any of us can ever explore than knowing God, according to the Scriptures.

Knowing God in Calvin's Theology
In Christian theology, knowing God has always been a key concept.

Two questions, of course, arise with regard to it: first, the question of content (what and how much can we know?), and second, the question of method (how and by what means does this knowledge come to us?). The rest of this book gives a partial answer to the first question; this chapter deals with the second. The best and most masterful among Christian expositors of this theme, in my view, was John Calvin, whose *Institutes of the Christian Religion* provide a classic treatment of biblical teaching on the knowledge of God. Part of what happened during the five editions of his book's growth, from the little pocket book that it was in 1536 to the big folio that it became in 1559, was that the theme of knowing God, dealt with sketchily in the first edition, indeed dismissed in scarcely more than a sentence, came to dominate the whole structure.

The opening sentence of the 1536 *Institutes* was this: "The sum of sacred doctrine is contained in these two parts: the knowledge of God and of ourselves." In the second edition that sentence was changed into this: "The sum of our wisdom is contained in our knowledge of God and of ourselves." From the second to the fourth edition, that sentence was then expanded in separate chapters: one on the knowledge of God, one on the knowledge of ourselves. In the final edition, the sum of Calvin's material was arranged in four distinct books. The first book was called *Of the Knowledge of God the Creator;* the second book was called *Of the Knowledge of Christ the Redeemer;* and the third was called *Of the Way to Come to Know the Grace of Christ.* The theme of knowing God expanded until it virtually controlled and shaped the whole work.

Calvin's teaching is, first, that the knowledge of God is more than the natural person's awareness of God. Calvin is very emphatic that all human beings are aware of God and, try as they might, cannot get rid of this awareness. Calvin calls this sense of deity the "seed of religion" that is planted in every human heart. The unredeemed person wishes to pretend that there is no God, but pretense it remains, because deep down he or she cannot help knowing that God is. Nonetheless, this awareness of God's reality is not to be equated with the knowledge of God that the Christian has, for, to Calvin, knowledge of God is always personal knowledge within a covenanted relationship, and non-Christians lack this. Only through the agency of our Lord Jesus Christ does such a relationship become a reality. As he himself said, "I am the way and the truth and the life. No one comes to the Father [that is, comes to know God as his or her heavenly Father] except through me" (Jn 14:6).

Knowledge of God as our covenant God, that is, as the Creator who has given himself to us to be our God of grace forever, is basic to Calvin's understanding because it is basic to the Bible's understanding of what knowing God means. "Religion," said Luther, "is a matter of personal pronouns," that is, it centers upon my being able to say to God, "My God," and knowing that God says to me, "My child." It is in and through that relationship that knowledge of God becomes the life-transforming reality that Calvin knew it to be.

Second, knowledge of God is more than any real or fancied experience of God. Calvin, like the Bible, is able to be very clear on this, for Calvin, like the Bible, is a product of an era when people were less self-absorbed than we are and were more interested in the realities we experience than in our experiences of them. It is rather difficult, I think, for us modern-day people to understand this distinction. We are very self-absorbed; the human-centeredness of our Western culture has made us so. We are interested in experiences, meaning our "feelings" or our "reactions to something," for their own sake, as if experiences are all that matter. We are inclined to jump to the conclusion that the more intense an experience is, the more of God there must be in it. But by biblical standards, that is not so at all.

Not even what is set forth as a conversion experience may be equated with the knowledge of God, for, says Scripture, we know God by faith. Faith is an outgoing of the heart in trust. Experiences flow from it, but faith is a relationship of recognition, credence and trust and is not in itself an experience. I grant that without faith there would be no conversion experiences. But faith is something distinct from any experience. Faith is the outgoing of our heart to God and Christ, who are there inviting us to themselves, saying to us, "Come and put your trust for eternal life in the Father and the Son." Faith focuses not on feelings but on facts, not on reactions inside us but on realities outside us, on the words and works of the God who is there, searching us, knowing us and personally addressing us, whether we like it or not. There are imitation experiences of God and of conversion that do not spring from real faith and are not instances of knowledge of God at all. This is something we must not forget.

Third, knowledge of God, according to Calvin and the Bible, is more than knowing *about* God, although knowing about God is its foundation. There is a difference between knowledge by description, in which you simply gain information about something, and knowledge by acquaintance, in which you are in direct contact with that reality. The knowledge of God is by acquaintance, which is more than knowledge by description. When it comes to knowledge by description, Calvin is very emphatic as to what must be known about God. In the first chapter of the first edition of the *Institutes,* Calvin wrote that there are four things that must be known about God. First, God is "infinite wisdom, righteousness, goodness, mercy, truth, power and life, so that there is no other wisdom, righteousness, goodness, mercy, truth, power and life save in him." Second, "All things, both in heaven and earth, were created to his glory." Third, "He is a righteous judge who sternly punishes those who swerve from his laws and do not wholly fulfill his will." And fourth, "He is mercy and gentleness, receiving kindly the rich and the poor who flee to his clemency and entrust themselves to his faithfulness." These are the basics we must know about God if we are ever to come to know him. But, says Calvin, to know these things and to have them clear in our minds is not yet to know God. For knowledge of God, *cognitio Dei,* is relational knowledge, knowledge that comes to us, as was said above, in the relationship of commitment, trust and reliance—in other words, of faith.

Then the fourth point is this. Knowing God is in fact more than knowing God. It involves knowing ourselves as needy creatures and lost sinners, for it is precisely a matter of knowing God in his saving relationship to us, that relationship in which he takes pity on us in our sinfulness and lovingly gives himself and his gifts to us for our renewal and enrichment. In other words, knowledge of God occurs only where there is knowledge of ourselves and our need and thankful reception of God's gifts to meet our need. Calvin is right! The knowledge of God and of ourselves—these two things together—does in truth make up the sum of our wisdom. In fact, we do not begin to know God until we know God's gracious gift of a Savior offered to us in our weakness, sin and wretchedness. For God is not a passive object that we can inspect and examine when and as we wish; he is an active subject who relates to us not on our terms but on his. And his terms are that we must be realistic about ourselves and approach him in conscious unworthiness, as drowning souls begging for a lifeline. Only to those who approach him so does he give himself covenantally and relationally. Only they, therefore, come to know God.

This brings us to the point where we can speak positively of what knowing God is, and we can now declare that knowing God by faith, according to the Scriptures, is three things together: it is *apprehension* of who and what he is; it is *application* to ourselves of what he gives; and it is *adoration* of him, the Giver. Let Calvin say this to us in his own terms: "The knowledge of God, as I understand it, is that by which we not only conceive, that is, form the concept of there being a God, but we also grasp what benefits us, what profits us, from his giving. Nor shall we say that God is, strictly speaking, known where there is no religion or godliness." Calvin delineates here the response of humble adoration and worship by lip, by heart and in life. Again,

Calvin says this: "We are called to a knowledge of God which does not just flit about in the brain," that is, rest content with bare notions and empty speculations. Knowledge of God, he says, is not merely a matter of ideas but is a knowledge that, if we rightly grasp it and allow it to take root in our hearts, will be "solid" and "fruitful." By "solid," he means firmly rooted and fixed; by "fruitful," he means "life-changing." So true knowledge of God means bringing forth the fruit of Christlikeness. Again he says: "The knowledge of God is not identified with cold speculation, but brings with it worship of him" (*Institutes* 1.2).

How Do We Know God?
This, then, is what knowing God meant to Calvin and what it means (so I am persuaded, as he was) in the Scriptures. But how does this knowledge of God come about? What are the means of our knowing God? The usual Christian formula is that knowledge of God depends upon God's special, gracious, saving revelation of himself to us—in other words, that our knowledge and God's revelation are correlative, the former deriving from the latter. That is right. Yet sometimes I find myself wishing that in place of that word *revelation* we could form the habit of substituting another word that I think in modern discussion and debate would express more. In place of "revelation" I would like to say "communication." The word *revelation* suggests to modern minds little more than a general display or exhibition of something. I believe it is very important, when we think of the revelation of God, always to keep in view its nature as personal communication from the Creator to his creatures.

Communication suggests someone approaching us, coming close to us, speaking to us, telling us about himself, opening his mind to us, giving us what he has, telling us what he knows, asking for our attention and seeking our response to what he is saying. This is the true idea of divine revelation, on which we must always keep our minds clear.

At this point, however, there is a specific problem at which we have hinted already. God made the human race in order that he might communicate himself to us and draw us into loving fellowship with himself. This was always his purpose. But we have turned away from God; sin has come in; human nature has become twisted. The human race is now radically anti-God in all its basic attitudes. The human race is not interested in fellowship with God. It is no longer in our nature to love God or to respond to God in any kind of worship. We have our back to God, we might say. In consequence of the Fall it is now human nature to do over and over what Adam and Eve are found doing in Genesis 3, that is, hiding from God so as to avoid having to face our guilt and so as to establish independence of him in the way we live.

We treat ourselves as though we were God. We live for ourselves; we are self-servers; we seek to bend everything to our own interests. In doing this we fight God—the real God. We say no to him. We push him away from the center of our life to its circumference. We keep him at bay because it is our nature to do that. So God's communication to us in our sin has to do more than simply present truth to our mind; it has to work in the human heart and alter fallen human nature.

Let us back up a moment. There is, says Calvin (and we have begun to see him saying this already), a universal self-communication by God, a divine activity usually called "general revelation," in the created order around us. And in our own nature, too, in our awareness of our own awesomely complex makeup and in the functioning of our consciences, there is revelation, that is, communication from God. Some sense of the reality of God and his claims comes through to us in the same way that an awareness of light comes through. It is immediate, pervasive, inescapable, undeniable.

Calvin is very strong on this. "God has so shown himself in the whole workmanship of this world that men cannot open their eyes without being forced to see him." Again, "The orderly arrangement of the world is like a mirror in which we may contemplate the otherwise invisible God." Once more: "The world is created for the display of God's glory." And "The world is the theater of God's glory." Again, "The Lord clearly displays both himself and his immortal kingdom in the mirror of his works." And yet again, "In the splendor of the heavens there is presented to our view a lively image of God" (*Institutes* 1.5.1-2).

The awareness of the Creator, then, comes through in all our commerce with his creatures, as it does in all our knowledge and awareness of ourselves and our own identity, in the judgments on us of our conscience, and in many of the thoughts of our own hearts. But humanity's way is to ignore or deny this awareness, or if we cannot deny it outright, to distort it and turn it into darkness and superstition. Thus the world, for all its fancied wisdom and multiple dreamed-up theologies, does not know God, even though this general communication of God through nature and inward experience is a reality for everyone. So says Calvin, following Paul (see Rom 1:18-23, 32; 2:12-16; 1 Cor 1:21). If, therefore, God is ever to be acknowledged, worshiped and trusted as he should be, he not only must set his truth before us but must also give us eyes to see it, ears to hear it and hearts to receive it. And that, in fact, is precisely his agenda.

Knowledge of God Through Grace
What God has done is to add to this general communication of himself in the natural order a special communication of himself in grace. In this process three stages need to be distinguished. Stage one was achieving *redemption in history.* By words and by works, God made himself known on the stage of history in saving action. The words were basic, for first God declared what he was going to do; then, after making the announcement, he acted, fulfilling his word and doing what he said. That is how it was at the exodus, when he saved Israel out of captivity in Egypt. That is what he did when in the fullness of

time he sent his own Son, born of a woman, to redeem those who were under the law, sinners like you and me, so that we might receive the gift of adoption and so become children in his family.

Stage two was recording *revelation in writing.* That was the work of God inspiring the Holy Scriptures. God caused to be written interpretive records of what he had said and done, so that all generations might know of the redemptive revelation in history that he had made. The written record is our Bible, which has Jesus Christ the Redeemer as its central focus.

The third stage in the communicative process is securing *reception by individuals* of the realities of redemption declared in the Scriptures, a reception that becomes a reality through the work of the Holy Spirit. God's word to the world is the message of new life in Christ. The Holy Spirit opens hearts to give this word entrance and renews hearts so that we might turn around again to face God. We thus become new creatures in Christ.

When the New Testament speaks of God revealing himself to human beings, it is this third stage in the process of divine communication that is in view. When Jesus said, "No one knows the Father except the Son and those to whom the Son chooses to reveal him" (Mt 11:27), he had in mind the enlightening impact of his teaching through the Holy Spirit. And it appears that when Jesus said, "Blessed are you, Simon son of Jonah, for this [my identity as God's Christ] was not revealed to you by man, but by my Father in heaven" (Mt 16:17), he meant that Simon had been enlightened to see the meaning of things he had heard Jesus say and seen him do during the previous months.

Paul uses the word *reveal* in the same way when he says in Galatians that God "was pleased to reveal his Son in me" (Gal 1:15-16). The Greek says "in me," that is, in a way that convinced Paul's heart. Paul lost his sight physically for a few days but gained his sight spiritually forever. The truth about Jesus, risen Savior and Lord, had been told to him before, but he had been blind to it; now the eyes of his heart were opened, and he saw. The same thought is expressed by Paul in other words when he says in 2 Corinthians 4:6 that "God, who said, 'Let light shine out of darkness,' made his light shine in our hearts to give us the light of the knowledge of the glory of God in the face of Christ."

Often this third stage of God's revelatory work is called illumination. John expresses it in words that we quoted earlier: "the Son of God . . . has given us understanding, so that we may know him who is true" (1 Jn 5:20).

Do you see now that stage two in the process, the inspiring of the Bible, is absolutely crucial? Calvin regularly referred to the Bible as the "oracles of God," a phrase found in Romans 3:2, which the NIV renders as "the very words of God." Calvin took it and used it again and again to express the thought that what we have in Scripture is God's own witness to his work of salvation. Calvin's view is that the Bible through the Spirit has a double function in relation to us sin-blinded sinners. It functions both as our schoolmaster, teaching us the truth, operating as the rule for our own teaching and speaking, and also as our spectacles, enabling us to see God clearly.

Calvin's illustration speaks much to me because I am nearsighted. If I take off my glasses, I cannot see anything or anyone clearly. I can see only a set of smudges. Calvin, who himself was nearsighted, says, in effect, that the natural man without the Scriptures has no more than a smudgy awareness that there is a divine something or someone there; he or she does not know who the something or the someone is. But, says Calvin, when nearsighted persons put on their glasses, they see clearly what before was only a smudge. Likewise, when we begin to study the Scriptures, we begin to see clearly him of whom we had that unclear awareness. The Scriptures serve us as glasses, focusing for us and in us our awareness of God and showing us precisely who and what this God is.

So Calvin opposes any form of theology that seeks to operate apart from the Scriptures. He denounces it as ungodly speculation and summons us to that humility that acknowledges need and is willing to be taught from the written word. Unfortunately, much theology today is speculative in the sense that he condemned. It patronizes the Scriptures; it stands above the Scriptures, going beyond and away from them. Such theology, no matter how learned, is trash, says Calvin. As one whose profession obliges him to spend a great deal of his time reading it, I can only endorse that opinion. All theology that moves away from the Scripture is basically trash, and one of the miseries of the modern church is that much of its literature, preaching and thinking is so much trash at this point.

What is called for now, as in Calvin's day, is the humility that bows before the Scriptures and accepts them as instruction from God. They are God preaching, God talking, God telling, God instructing, God setting before us the right way to think and speak about him. The Scriptures are God showing us himself: God communicating to us who he is and what he has done so that in the response of faith we may truly know him and live our lives in fellowship with him. Interpreting Scripture is often said to be a problem, but those who read the Bible as God's teaching, given in the form and through the means of human teaching, will find its message constantly coming through clearly— often more clearly than is comfortable. Then the question is not whether we understand but whether we are going to believe and obey.

John Wesley, the founder of Methodism, put it this way: "I am a creature of a day . . . hovering over the great gulf; till . . . I drop into an unchangeable eternity! I want to know one thing, the way to heaven. . . . God himself has . . . written it down in a book. O give me that book! At any price, give me the book of God! I have it. Here is knowledge enough for me. . . . I sit down alone: only God is here. In his presence I . . . read his book . . . to find the way to heaven. . . . I lift up my heart to the Father of Lights: 'Lord . . . let me know thy will.' " Do you identify with that? Do you go along with John Wesley in his attitude to his Bible as a supreme gift of God's grace? This Word is what the world must have if it is ever to know God. Thank God for it, then, and value and prize it.

At the coronation of the sovereign of England, the moderator of the Church of Scotland presents him or her with a Bible and speaks of it as—I quote the words exactly—"the most valuable thing that this world affords. Here is wisdom," he continues; "this is the royal Law; these are the lively oracles of God." That is utterly true, and so we may say that Christ and the Scriptures belong together as twin gifts of the grace of God. Authentic theology begins here, in recognition of this truth and in glad submission to the teaching of Scripture, from which we learn of our Savior and the path of eternal life. Authentic knowledge of God begins here, too, and the following chapters will spell out some of its contents as the Bible presents them.

2

REVELATION &
AUTHORITY

B UILT INTO CHRISTIANITY AND BOUND UP WITH THE IDEA OF knowing God through his Word is the principle of authority. Christianity, as we have seen, is a revealed religion. It claims that God has acted to make known his mind and will, and that his revelation has authority for our lives. Biblical religion is marked by certainty about beliefs and duties. The diffidence and indefiniteness of conviction that thinks of itself as humility has no place or warrant in Scripture, where humility begins with taking God's word about things. All through the Bible God's servants appear as folk who know what God has told them and are living by that knowledge. This is true of patriarchs, prophets, psalmists, apostles and other, lesser lights, and is supremely true of the Lord Jesus Christ himself.

Authority in the Life of Christ
Let us focus on Christ for a moment. He was the Son of God incarnate and as such had no will of his own. It was his nature, as well as his duty and delight, to do his Father's will in everything. He is on record

as having said, "I do nothing on my own but speak just what the Father has taught me. . . . I always do what pleases him" (Jn 8:28-29; compare 4:34; 5:30; 6:38; 8:26; 12:49-50; 14:31; 17:4). Jesus knew that his authority as his Father's messianic agent depended on his remaining subject to the Father in this way. (He commended the Roman centurion for seeing that [Matthew 8:10].)

That he was in his Father's will was to Jesus a source of tremendous strength, as became very plain in the last week of his earthly life. One day he rode into Jerusalem at the head of a cheering crowd like a king coming to be crowned. The next day, alone, he went through the temple like a hurricane, wrecking the bazaar in the Court of the Gentiles, kicking out the stall holders, upsetting the bankers' desks and dazzling onlookers by the fury with which he denounced the business routines he had thus disrupted. The authorities huddled. Two big demonstrations in two days! What for? And what next? The day after, "while Jesus was walking in the temple courts, the chief priests, the teachers of the law and the elders came to him. 'By what authority are you doing these things?' they asked" (Mk 11:27-28). Jesus replied, in effect, that his authority was like that of John's baptism. It was from God. He was doing his Father's will and knew it, as he showed again two days later in Gethsemane: "Not as I will, but as you will. . . . Your will be done. . . . It must happen in this way" (Mt 26:39, 42, 54). His Father's will was the shaper of all his life.

Jesus was divine. We are not. So it might be expected that Jesus' followers would be less certain about the Father's mind and will than he was. In the New Testament, however, it is not so, whatever may be true of some professed Christians today. *Know* is a New Testament keyword; "we know" is a New Testament refrain. The writers of the New Testament claim that Christians know God, his work, his will and his ways because they have received revelation from him. They tell us that God's self-revelation has taken the form not only of action but also of instruction. God, so they say, has spoken in and through what

Jesus said (Heb 1:1-4; 2:3). He has made known to apostles and prophets the secret of his eternal plan (Eph 1:9-10; 3:3-11; compare Rom 16:25-26; 1 Cor 2:6-11). Apostolic preachers relay his message "not in words taught . . . by human wisdom but in words taught by the Spirit" (1 Cor 2:13). We receive this as "sound doctrine" (2 Tim 4:3; Tit 1:9; 2:1), "the truth" (2 Thess 2:10, 12-13, and so on), "the word of God" (1 Thess 2:13, and so on). We thus gain sure and certain knowledge of God's mind. Modern theology will oppose the authority of Christ to that of Scripture, but in the New Testament, bowing to Christ's lordship and believing God-taught doctrine entail each other.

Believing and Obedience

Believing must lead to obedience. Christians have constantly been in trouble for defying human authorities and challenging consensuses. Peter would not stop evangelizing when told to (Acts 4:19-20; 5:27-42) and was in and out of prison as a result. Christians risked persecution in the early days by refusing the formalities of Roman state religion, just as latter-day African Christians have courted martyrdom by rejecting tribal rites. Athanasius sentenced himself to exile by standing against the Arian world in the fourth century. Luther jeopardized his life by refusing to recant at the court of Worms in sixteenth-century Germany. Christians today make themselves unpopular by opposing such social realities as the pornography trade and such social conveniences as abortion on demand. These are samples of the costly nonconformity that Christians have practiced down the ages.

Why do Christ's disciples behave so outrageously? Because, standing under God's authority, they are sure that his revelation requires them to act as they do at whatever personal cost. Luther said at Worms, "My conscience is captive to the Word of God; to go against conscience is neither right nor safe; here I stand, there is nothing else I can do; God help me; amen." The privilege of knowing God's truth with certainty and precision carries with it the responsibility of obeying that truth with equal precision. Christianity is no armchair faith but a call to action.

The Problem of Authority

But here a difficulty arises: whose version of revealed truth should be accepted? Imagine the perplexity of the Galatian Christians the day they first had read to them the blistering sentences in which Paul goes after some who "are trying to pervert the gospel of Christ" (Gal 1:7) in part by championing circumcision as a spiritual necessity. "As for those agitators, I wish they would go the whole way and emasculate themselves!" (Gal 5:12). Imagine, too, how the Colossian Christians must have gulped when they first heard the words of Paul (whom they had never met) cutting down the teacher who was delighting in "false humility and the worship of angels" and who was puffed up "with idle notions" (Col 2:18). In each case Paul was squelching respected men whose teaching on faith and duty had hitherto been treated as true. Whom should they follow—Paul or their local pundits?

This problem is still with us. Roman Catholics, for example, say that Christians should treat the pope as chief pastor of all Christendom and that his *ex cathedra* pronouncements, along with those of the church's councils, are infallible. They say that Christians should pray to Mary and see the Eucharist as in some sense the church's sacrifice for its sins. With this Protestants disagree. Again, Protestant radicals deny Jesus' personal deity, objective sin-bearing, bodily resurrection and personal return. With this the great body of both Protestants and Catholics disagree. What, now, should the plain Christian do when he or she finds fellow believers at odds about the truth and will of God, some saying one thing, some another? What procedure should be followed in order to determine one's own belief and behavior? Three alternatives are available to us.

1. The church as final authority. Some people treat the consensus of the church as decisive, making ecclesiastical tradition and consensus their authoritative guides to the authoritative will of God. This is what the Roman Catholic and Eastern Orthodox churches, with some Anglicans, tell us we should do. The implications of this rule of procedure will vary for individuals according to what they mean by *church* (church of Rome, early church, their own denomination or whatever), but the principle is clear. You should approach the Bible as a product of the church and equate mainstream church teaching with the biblical faith. You should study Scripture by the light of that teaching and make Scripture fit in with it. Where the church has not pronounced, you may freely speculate, but you should take as from God all the definite teaching the church gives. What the church says, God says. Therefore, the Holy Spirit's first step in teaching us is to make us docile under church authority.

2. *The individual as final authority.* Other people may, by contrast, treat their own ideas as decisive, whatever dissent from the Bible and the historic church that may involve. With this view, Scripture and church teaching are essentially resource material to help us make up our own minds. Both should be known, but neither need be endorsed, in this view, for neither is infallible and both include chaff as well as wheat. The theologies found in Scripture and Christian history are uneven attempts to verbalize a religious awareness in such terms as different cultures provided, and each is a mixture of facts and fancies, insights and mistakes. Our task is to sort out what seems lastingly valid and express that in contemporary terms. The implied principle is that what our own spirit says (that is, what our reason, conscience and imagination come up with under the stimulus of the Bible and the church's historic ideas), God says. The Holy Spirit's work is to sensitize our spirit for the task of picking, choosing, selecting, correcting and adjusting the witness of Scripture and tradition in whatever way we think right.

3. *The Bible as final authority.* A third viewpoint is that the Christian must treat Holy Scripture as decisive, according to the dictum of the

seventeenth-century Westminster Confession: "The supreme judge by which all controversies of religion are to be determined, and all decrees of councils, opinions of ancient writers, doctrines of men, and private spirits, are to be examined, and in whose sentence we are to rest, can be no other but the Holy Spirit speaking in the Scripture" (1.10). One who takes this line departs from the second view by receiving the Bible as God's authoritative instruction for all time, and from the first view by subjecting the church's teaching and interpretations to the judgment of the Bible itself as a self-interpreting whole. He or she will look to the Holy Spirit, who gave the Scriptures, to authenticate their contents to God's people as God's truth and to show how this truth applies to life (compare 1 Jn 2:20, 27). The believer's constant aim will be to have Scripture judge and correct all human ideas, including his or her own. The believer will value the church's doctrinal and expository heritage but not give it the last word. The believer's heart will echo Augustine's breathtaking words to God: "What your Scripture says, you say." Believers will view the Spirit's teaching role as, first and foremost, one of keeping our minds humbly and eagerly attuned to Scripture, the divine textbook, so that we are willing to have Scripture change our minds where it finds us wrong.

To illustrate how these alternatives might work, let us imagine a debate about abortion on demand. An adherent of the first approach (call him a traditionalist or an ecclesiasticist) would oppose the practice because the church has always forbidden it. An adherent of the third approach (call her a biblicist or an evangelical) would oppose the practice because Scripture forbids killing people and will not let us see the fetus as anything less than a person heading for a viable life. The adherent of the second approach (call him a subjectivist or a relativist), however, might well dismiss the biblical and churchly view of the fetus as unscientific and prohibitions based on it as groundless and inappropriate. He might defend abortion on demand as compassionate to women, urging that unwanted babies are a bad thing and that modern medical technology makes the operation fairly safe. He thus takes his ideas not from the Bible or the church but from the world around him.

Among these alternative methods of determining God's will you and I must choose. They are not compatible methods, even when on particular points (say, on the desirability of some form of democracy in the state, or the need for pastoral care in the church) all three yield coinciding convictions. The first and the third, which both view Scripture as revealed truth that abides, are closer to each other than either is to the second, which treats biblical thought as a transient cultural product. Yet the gap between even these two is wide, as the historic tension between Roman Catholicism and evangelical Protestantism shows. Individuals may and do bounce inconsistently among the three alternatives, but each in itself excludes the two others.

Which method, then, is right? Which is authentically Christian? Which squares with the teaching and purpose of Christ and his apostles? Which would Jesus and Paul and John and Peter approve, were they back with us today to guide us? I think the answer is plain.

Christ's View of Authority

Take Jesus first. There is no good reason to doubt the authenticity of what the Gospels say of him. They were evidently written in good faith and with great care by knowledgeable persons (see Lk 1:1-4; Jn 19:35; 21:24). They were composed at a time when Jesus was still remembered and misstatements about him could be nailed. They were accepted everywhere, it seems, as soon as they were known, though the early Christians were not credulous and detected spurious gospels with skill. The consensus of the centuries has been that these four portraits of Jesus have a ring of truth. It is easy to believe that so awesome and unconventional a figure as Jesus, with his divine self-awareness and claims, would be well remembered; he would, indeed, prove unforgettable. By contrast, it is beyond belief that such a figure would be no more than the product of overheated imaginations. We may be confident that in reading the Gospels we meet the real Jesus. From them, now, we learn the following facts.

Jesus' own authority. Jesus claimed absolute personal authority in all his teaching: "It was said . . . but I tell you . . ." (Mt 5:21-22, 27-28, 31-34, 38-39, 43-44); "he taught as one who had authority, and not as their teachers of the law" (Mt 7:29); "heaven and earth will pass away, but my words will never pass away" (Mk 13:31). He said that our destiny depends on whether, having heard his words, we heed them or not (Mt 7:24-27; Lk 6:47-49): "There is a judge for the one who rejects me and does not accept my words; that very word which I spoke will condemn him at the last day. For I did not speak of my own accord, but the Father who sent me commanded me what to say and how to say it. . . . So whatever I say is just what the Father has told me to say" (Jn 12:48-50).

Old Testament authority. Jesus taught the absolute divine authority of the Jewish Scriptures. Some two hundred references in the Gospels combine to make his view of our Old Testament crystal clear. He saw the books as having both human authors and a divine author, so that, for example, commands that Moses presents as the word of God are indeed such (Mk 7:8-13), and an expository comment in Genesis 2:24 can be quoted as what "the Creator . . . said" (Mt 19:4). As God's Word, disclosing his truth, purpose and command, Scripture has abiding authority (Mt 5:18-20; Jn 10:35).

It is striking to see how Jesus, while setting his personal authority against that of earlier rabbinic interpreters (which is what he was doing when he contrasted what "was said" with what "I tell you"), always bowed and taught others to bow to Scripture as such. He gave the key to his whole ministry when he said, "Do not think that I have come to abolish the Law or the Prophets; I have not come to abolish them but to fulfill them" (Mt 5:17), that is, to be fully subject to them as they applied to him. From Scripture he resolved questions of doctrine (the certainty of resurrection, Mark 12:24-27; the intended permanence of marriage, Matthew 19:5-6) and ethics (the rightness of letting need override sabbath restrictions, Matthew 12:2-8; the wrongness of legalism as a cop-out from the obligations of the fifth commandment, Mark 7:10-13). By Scripture he justified the acts of his ministry (cleansing the temple, Mark 11:15-17). By it he discerned his personal calling to be the Servant-Messiah who must enter upon his reign by the path of death and resurrection (Mt 26:53-56; Mk 12:10-11; 14:21; Lk 18:31; 22:37; 24:25-27, 44-49; compare Mt 4:4, 7, 10). So, having taught and enforced Scripture throughout his ministry, he went up to Jerusalem to obey Scripture by being killed there. No stronger witness to the authority of Scripture, even for the Son of God, could be given. To him it was all God's word, and whatever it foretold must be fulfilled.

Jesus' resurrection was his vindication, the Father's seal of approval set publicly on all the Son had said and done, including what he said about Scripture and his going to Jerusalem to die in obedience to Scripture. It is surely significant that on resurrection day he appeared to two groups of disciples to explain how Scripture had been fulfilled in his dying and rising to reign (Lk 24:25-27, 44-47). It is also, of course, significant that Luke tells these stories so fully and carefully; he is anxious that his readers should see their point.

New Testament authority. Jesus conferred his own authority on the apostles to go out in his name as his witnesses and spokesmen. In appointing them his messengers, Jesus promised them the Spirit to enable them to fulfill their task (Mk 13:11; Lk 24:47-49; Jn 14:25-26; 15:26-27; 16:7-15; 20:21-23; Acts 1:8), and he prayed for all his people, present and future, in just two categories: first, the apostles; second, "those who will believe in me *through their message*" (Jn 17:20, emphasis added). Thus he showed that the apostles' witness would be both the norm and the means of all other Christians' faith to the end of time. Permanent availability requires writing, so this was virtually a promise of a New Testament to come.

Apostolic Authority

The rest of the New Testament is as we would expect in light of these facts. On the one hand, the apostles are conscious of their role as Christ's commissioned representatives and of the God-givenness and divine authority of their teaching. This is especially clear in Paul and John, who both addressed situations where their authority had been challenged. In 1 Corinthians 2:12 and following verses, Paul claims both inward illumination and verbal inspiration for his message. In 1 Corinthians 14:37 and 2 Thessalonians 3:6, he insists that his directives must be taken as commands of the Lord whom he represents. In Galatians 1:8-9, he solemnly curses anyone who brings a message different from his own.

John calmly but breathtakingly states in black and white, "We [apostolic witnesses] are from God, and whoever knows God listens to us; but whoever is not from God does not listen to us. This is how we recognize the Spirit of truth and the spirit of falsehood" (1 Jn 4:6). Bolder authority claims could hardly be made. The apostles are no less sure than were the Old Testament prophets that their message was from God.

But on the other hand, with equal emphasis they claim the Jewish Scriptures as divine instruction for Christians, prophetically proclaiming Christ, the gospel and the realities of discipleship to the church. "The holy Scriptures . . . are able to make you wise for salvation through faith in Christ Jesus. All Scripture is God-breathed and is useful for teaching, rebuking, correcting and training in righteousness, so that the man of God may be thoroughly equipped for every good work" (2 Tim 3:15-17). Of what he calls "the prophetic writings" or "the oracles of God," Paul declares, "Everything that was written in the past was written to teach us, so that through endurance and the encouragement of the Scriptures we [Christians] might have hope" (Rom 15:4; compare 1 Cor 10:11). Old Testament passages are quoted as God's own speech in Acts (4:25-26; 28:25-27) and Hebrews (3:7-

11; 10:15-17). Further, Paul's phrases "the Scripture says to Pharaoh" (Rom 9:17) and "the Scripture foresaw . . . and announced the gospel in advance to Abraham" (Gal 3:8) show how completely he himself equated Scripture with God speaking—we might even say, God preaching. That the Jewish Scriptures have God's plan concerning Christ as their main subject is everywhere taken for granted. In Hebrews the deity, humanity and mediation of Christ are the doctrinal themes, and every point up to the start of chapter thirteen is made by expounding and applying the Old Testament. The New Testament view of the Old is consistent and clear.

So the Jewish Scriptures were held to be an authoritative, God-given witness to Christ, just as was apostolic preaching. In both cases the authority was seen not as human, the relative yet uneven authority of insight and expertise, but as divine, the absolute, oracular authority of God telling truth about his work and his will, and about the worship and obedience that we owe him. Not all that was said, whether by the Old Testament or by the apostles, was equally important, but all was part of the rule of faith and life since it came from God.

Since Jewish Scripture and apostolic preaching were on a par, it was as natural as it was momentous that Peter, having reminded his readers that Old Testament Scripture came as "men . . . were carried along by the Holy Spirit" (2 Pet 1:21), then equated Paul's sermons on paper (which is what his letters were) with "the other Scriptures" (3:16) and admonished his readers to heed both and not mishandle either. Here the Christian authority principle at last becomes explicit: the Old Testament read in conjunction with the apostolic presentation of Christ (or putting it the other way around, the apostolic presentation of Christ conjoined with the Old Testament) is the rule of faith for Jesus' disciples. God now teaches, reproves, corrects and instructs in and by what is written in the two Testaments together.

Despite the newness of the New Testament, the principle that the written Word of God must shape faith and life was old. The basis of

Old Testament religion was that God had spoken in human language and had caused his teaching to be recorded for all time, and that the way to please him was to go by the book. All Jesus' teaching and ministry assumed this. What follows, then? Should we say that he founded Christianity on a fallacy? Or should we not rather say that by endorsing this basic Jewish tenet he showed that it was true?

Here we reach a crucial point for our own faith. So far we have been appealing to the Bible simply as a good historical source, from which we may learn with certainty what the founders of Christianity taught. But if Jesus was God incarnate and spoke with personal divine authority, and if by sending the Spirit he really enabled his apostles to speak God's word with total consistency, it follows that both Testaments (that which his Spirit produced as well as that which he knew and authenticated) ought to be received as "the very words of God" and as "God-breathed and . . . useful . . . so that the man of God may be thoroughly equipped" (Rom 3:2; 2 Tim 3:16-17). Only as we seek to believe and do what the two Testaments tell us do we have the full right to call ourselves Jesus' disciples. "Why do you call me, 'Lord, Lord,' and do not do what I say?" (Lk 6:46). Scripture comes to us, as it were, from Jesus' hand, and its authority and his are so interlocked as to be one.

Bowing to the living Lord, then, entails submitting mind and heart to the written Word. Disciples individually and churches corporately stand under the authority of Scripture because they stand under the lordship of Christ, who rules by Scripture. This is not bibliolatry but Christianity in its most authentic form.

Biblical Authority

So we learn from Christ to learn from Scripture as God's authoritative Word. We may spell out the theology of that lesson as follows.

The Creator communicates. God made us in his image, rational and responsive, so that he and we might live in fellowship. To this end, he makes himself known to us. He enters into communication with a view to communion. Always he has caused his works of creation and providence to mediate some sense of his reality, righteousness and glory to all who are alive in his world, however little they welcome this. "Since the creation of the world God's invisible qualities—his eternal power and divine nature—have been clearly seen, being understood from what has been made" (Rom 1:20; compare 1:32; 2:14-15; Acts 14:16-17; Ps 19:1-6). Moreover, God speaks in words, using his own gift of language to tell us about himself. We read that verbal revelation began in Eden before humanity fell (Gen 2:16-17) and that all that God has made known for salvation was revealed verbally to and through patriarchs, prophets, apostles and Jesus Christ, after which it was embodied in the Bible (Rom 15:4; Gal 3:8; Eph 3:4-5; Heb 2:3; 1 Pet 1:10-12).

God reveals salvation. The general formula is that God reveals himself so that people may know him. The specific formula is that God reveals himself as Savior so that sinners may know him savingly. Saving revelation, as in part we have seen already, is a fourfold divine activity, as follows.

First and most basic was God's historical self-disclosure by redemptive deeds preceded and followed by explanatory words, a sequence of acts that began with the patriarchs and the exodus and reached its climax in the messianic ministry, atoning death and triumphant resurrection of Jesus. In this, as Zechariah sang, God "raised up a horn of salvation for us in the house of his servant David" (Lk 1:69). The good news of these acts is the gospel.

Second and distinct from this was God's work of inspiring expository, celebratory and applicatory records of his words and deeds, so that all might know what he had done and would do, and what their response should be. The collection of these records is the Bible.

The third strand in God's revelatory work is his providential action in bringing to each individual's notice what Holy Scripture has made public and permanently available. He does this through his messengers who by whatever means spread the Good News. The generic name for this activity, which includes all forms of publication and instruction and is meant to involve all God's people, is proclamation, or preaching.

Fourth and following on from the third is the giving of understanding so that those instructed come to believe the message and commit themselves to the Savior who is its subject. This inner enlightening is called revelation in Matthew 11:27 and 16:17 and Galatians 1:16, as we saw earlier, but the usual name for it is illumination, according to the imagery of 2 Corinthians 4:6 and Ephesians 1:17-21.

All four modes of divine action—redemptive revelation in history, didactic revelation in Scripture, relayed revelation in the church's preaching and teaching, and illuminative revelation in the hearer's heart—are necessary if we are to know God as Savior through Christ. The first two modes ceased in the first century A.D., but the third and fourth continue. The fourth is necessary because although the Bible message authenticates itself as God's truth by the light and power that flow from it, fallen individuals are unresponsive and indeed resistant to it, so that without illumination the gospel will only be doubted, devalued and finally ignored (Lk 14:15-24; 2 Cor 4:3-4). God must enable us to see what he has revealed to the world in Jesus Christ, or else we will remain blind to it.

God's Spirit teaches through Scripture. The Spirit of Christ who indwells Christians never leads them to doubt, criticize, go beyond or fall short of biblical teaching. Spirits that do that are not the Spirit of Christ (1 Jn 4:1-6). Rather, the Spirit makes us appreciate the divine authority of Scripture, so that we accept its account of spiritual realities and live as it calls us to do. As the Spirit gave the Word by brooding over its human writers and leading the church to recognize their books as its canon for belief and behavior, so now he becomes the authoritative interpreter of Scripture as he shows us how biblical teaching bears on our living. To be sure, what Bible books meant as messages to their first readers can be gleaned to some extent from commentaries. But what they mean for our lives today is something we learn only as the Spirit stirs our insensitive consciences.

Never does the Spirit draw us away from the written Word, any more than from the living Word. Instead, the Spirit keeps us in constant, conscious, contented submission to both together. He exerts his authority precisely by making real to us the authority of Christ and of Scripture—more precisely, the authority of Christ through Scripture. This is what it means to be Spirit-led.

Scripture promotes ethics. Some fear that full acceptance of biblical authority must result in a legalistic lifestyle. The root of their fear seems to be a belief that God's law in Scripture really is a code of mechanical, impersonal dos and don'ts—in other words, that the Pharisees' view of the law was essentially right.

But Jesus' scorching comments on the Pharisees show that this view is wrong. The truth is that the moral teaching of Scripture focuses on the ideal of creative goodness that Jesus Christ actually lived out. It requires us not just to stay within the limits of specific commands and prohibitions but to stay within those limits so that we can make the best of every situation and relationship for the glory of God and the good of others. Lawkeeping must be love in action. This is the one truth embedded in the otherwise false scheme of "situation ethics," which refuses to accept the law laid down in Scripture as the teaching of God. The ethical creativity that is always asking what is the best we can do is one dimension of that Christlike holiness to which we are called, and those who believe most strongly in the authority of Scripture should be manifesting more of this quality than anyone else.

Scripture controls Christian consciences. Consciences not governed by God's Word are to that extent not Christian. "God alone is Lord of the conscience and hath left it free from the doctrines and commandments of men, which are, in any thing, contrary to his Word," says the Westminster Confession (20.2). One thinks again of Luther's statement at Worms: "My conscience is captive to the Word of God: to go against conscience is neither right nor safe." If conforming to ecclesiastical, governmental, marital or parental demands involves action contrary to Scripture, God can be served only by nonconformity at that point. This may put us out of step with others and prove costly to us, but nothing less will please God. Conversely, when we find Scripture requiring of us goals and standards that are not the way of the world (going the second mile, turning the other cheek, loving our enemies), we may not excuse ourselves by reflecting that nobody else behaves like that.

"Do not conform any longer to the pattern of this world," wrote Paul, "but be transformed by the renewing of your mind. Then you will be able to test and approve what God's will is—his good, pleasing and perfect will" (Rom 12:2). The phrase "test and approve" represents one Greek word, signifying the discernment of a consecrated conscience applying the generalities of God's Word to the specifics of one's personal life.

Scripture and Freedom

We saw earlier that true freedom is found only under God's authority. What we are seeing now is that it is found only under the authority of Scripture. Through Scripture, God's authority is mediated to people, and Christ by his Spirit rules his people's lives. Biblical authority is often expounded in opposition to lax views of truth. Not so often, however, is it presented as the liberating, integrating, invigorating principle that it really is. The common idea is that unqualified confidence in the Bible leads to narrow-minded inhibitions and crippling restraints on what you may think and do. The truth is that such confidence produces liberated living—living, that is, which is free from uncertainty, doubt and despair—that otherwise is not found anywhere. The one who trusts the Bible knows what God did, does and will do, what God commands and what God promises. With the Colossians, the Bible believer understands "God's grace in all its truth" (Col 1:6), for the Christ of Scripture has become his or her Savior, master and friend.

3

WHO IS GOD?

WHAT DOES IT MEAN TO SAY "GOD"? MANY TODAY WOULD have to answer this question as Augustine did when asked for a definition of time: "When I am not asked, I know very well; but when I am asked, I do not know at all!"

The doctrine of God is a confused area in Western theology. Each of its three departments—the divine attributes, the Trinity, and God's relation to the world—is disputed territory. This is basically because agreement is lacking as to how the doctrine should be constructed and defended. Different intellectual methods for doing this naturally produce different theological results.

Some theological words need to be learned before we plunge into this discussion. *Theism* means belief in a Creator who in providence fills and guides the world he made. *Deism* means belief in a Creator who has withdrawn from his world. *Pantheism* means belief in the identity of God and the universe, so that God minus the universe equals nothing. *Panentheism* means belief in a God who permeates everything and whose life is a matter of interacting with that which is not himself in a way that is less than omnipotent and sometimes unsuccessful. The Bible directs us to theism and away from the other ideas.

Hybrids often prove unstable, and the Western heritage of theism began as a hybrid. It grew out of the apologetic theology of the early centuries, in which much was made of the thought that Greco-Roman philosophy was a providential preparation for the gospel. This version of theism, which found its fullest statement when Thomas Aquinas (1225–1274) formulated it in Aristotelian terms, was a blend of reasoning from philosophy and the Bible, the former appearing to provide the frame into which the latter was then forced to fit. Opinions differ as to whether this method of formulating theism makes distortions of Bible truth unavoidable or not.

In this century some aspects of theism in its traditional form have become widely suspect among mainstream theologians. Certainly some rethinking is called for, but what we need is minor modification, not abandonment of traditional theism. This will become clear, I think, as we proceed.

The Anatomy of Theism

It will help us to review the ingredients that make up historic Christian theism. Here is a checklist of the usual items, expressed in as simple a way as the thoughts allow.

God is personal and triune. God is always Three-in-One and One-in-Three. All three are equal in power and glory, and in all divine acts all three persons are involved. God is as truly three personal centers in a relationship of mutual love as he is a single personal deity. *He* when used of God means *they*—the Father, the Son and the Holy Spirit.

God is self-existent and self-sufficient. God does not have it in him, either in purpose or in power, to stop existing. He exists necessarily. The answer to the child's question "Who made God?" is that God did not need to be made, since he was always there. He depends on nothing outside himself but is at every point self-sustaining.

God is simple, perfect and immutable. This means he is wholly and totally involved in everything that he is and does. His nature, goals, plans and ways of acting do not change, either for the better (being perfect, he cannot become better than he is) or for the worse.

God is infinite, without body, all-present, all-knowing and eternal. God is not bound by any of the limitations of space or time that apply to us, his creatures, in our body-anchored existence. Instead, he is always present everywhere, though invisibly and imperceptibly. He is at every moment cognizant of everything that ever was, now is or will be.

God is purposeful and all-powerful. He has a plan for the history of the universe, and in executing it he governs and controls all created realities. Without violating the nature of things and without at any stage infringing upon human free will, God acts in, with and through his creatures to do everything that he wishes to do exactly as he wishes to do it. By this sovereign, overruling action, he achieves his goals.

God is both transcendent over and immanent in his world. On the one hand, he is distinct from the world, does not need it and exceeds the grasp of any created intelligence that is found in it. On the other hand, he permeates the world in sustaining and creative power, shaping and steering it in a way that keeps it on its planned course.

God is impassible. This means that no one can inflict suffering, pain or any sort of distress on him. Insofar as God enters into an experience of suffering, it is through empathy for his creatures and according to his own deliberate decision. He is never his creatures' victim. This impassibility has not been taken by the Christian mainstream to mean that God is a stranger to joy and delight; rather, it asserts the permanence of God's joy, which no pain, however real, can cloud.

God is love. Giving out of goodwill, for the recipient's benefit, is the abiding quality both of ongoing relationships within the Trinity and of God's relationship with his creatures. This love is qualified by holiness (purity), a further facet of God's character that finds expression in his abhorrence and rejection of moral evil.

God is eternally worthy of our praise, loyalty and love. God's ways with humankind, as set forth in Scripture, show him to be both awesome and worthy of adoration by reason of his truthfulness, faithfulness, grace, mercy, patience, constancy, wisdom, justice, goodness and generosity. The ultimate purpose of human life is to render to him worship and service, in which both he and we will find joy. This is what we were made for and what we are saved for. This is what it means to know God and to be known by him and to glorify him.

God communicates to his creatures. God uses his gift of language, given to the human race, to tell us things directly in and through the words of his spokespersons—prophets, apostles, the incarnate Son, the writers of Holy Scripture and those who preach the Bible. God's messages all come to us as good news of grace. They may contain particular commands, even threats or warnings, but the fact that God addresses us at all is an expression of his goodwill and an invitation to fellowship. The central message of Scripture, the hub of the wheel whose spokes are the various truths about God that the Bible teaches, is and always will be God's unmerited gift of salvation, freely offered to us in and by Jesus Christ.

Traditional Theism Under Fire

What are the present-day problems with this venerable understanding of God? They have to do with its sources and method.

The positions themselves, as stated above, are plainly biblical. But the Platonist-Augustinian-Thomist tradition of philosophical theism has persistently held that knowledge of God's reality, and of several of the above facts about him, can and should be gleaned by rational analysis apart from the Bible's witness. This is where the uncertainty centers.

The influential twentieth-century theologian Karl Barth (1886–1968), in the powerful, Bible-based reassertions of trinitarian theism in his *Church Dogmatics*, spurned the help of this kind of "natural" theology. This did more than any other twentieth-century contribution to produce a pendulum swing against attempts to wed theology to philosophy. To be concerned lest philosophy becomes the dominant partner in this marriage is right and proper. Barth, however, wanted to go further and divorce them—a different agenda altogether.

Barth himself would use philosophical concepts as tools to help investigate biblical teaching. But he would not let these concepts become grids, limiting in advance what God is free to say to us through Scripture. Barth's protest, though justified within limits, threw the doctrine of God into great confusion. It opened the door to a selective reading of the Bible, free of coherent rational control and operating without regard for any of the traditional fixed points. That is what we face today in many quarters. The pendulum still swings between Thomist and Barthian extremes and shows no sign of coming to rest.

Karl Barth's Theism

Barth's contribution, though disruptive in others' hands in the manner just described, paved the way for some clarifications of the doctrine of God that we badly need.

Granted, his attack on natural theology—that is, the recognition that our existence and God's have something in common—was overdone. Granted, too, Barth's denial of general revelation through the created order was a mistake. (His refusal to recognize general revelation, apart from the gospel, in Romans 1:18-32 and 2:9-16, seems little short of perverse.)

Nevertheless, his polemic against the claim of natural theology, to establish for us foundation truths about God as a kind of runway for revelation, now appears as a largely justified attack on nineteenth-century attempts to domesticate God. (Barth's break with liberal theology began around 1915, when prominent German theologians blithely spoke of "using" the Christian faith "for purposes of conducting" World War I.) And Barth's insistence that all our doctrine of God must come from the Bible was healthy and right.

So it will not be enough to dismiss Barth as eccentric and then slump back into traditional postures and parrotings. If Barth, with his type of biblicism, did not do well enough, we must try with ours to do better. To that end I now venture some comments on the doctrine of God as today's evangelicals have received it.

Three Important Purgings

There are three important respects in which the traditional doctrine needs purging. It needs to be purged of elements of natural theology, elements of mystification and elements of rationalism. Let me explain.

Elements of natural theology need to be purged. Contrary to Barth, I affirm that general revelation is a fact, and its impact will again and again produce thoughts about God that, so far as they go, are right. As an example, Paul cites the non-Christian poets Epimenides and Aratus in Acts 17:28. Many are confident that rational apologetics (a form of natural theology) can, under God, trigger and crystallize such thoughts and insights. Unlike Barth, I see no reason to doubt their confidence. Yet I contend that natural theology needs to be eliminated from our attempts at theological construction. There are five reasons for this.

First, we do not need natural theology for information. Everything that natural theology, operating upon general revelation, can discern about the Creator and his ways is republished for us in those very Scriptures that refer to the general revelation of these things (see Ps 19; Acts 14:17; 17:27-28; Rom 1:18-32; 2:9-16). And Scripture, which we rightly receive on the grounds that it is God's own word of testimony and law, is a better source of knowledge about God than natural theology can ever be.

Second, we do not strengthen our position by invoking natural theology. On the contrary, claiming that biblical truths rest on philosophical foundations can only give the impression that the biblical message about God's redemption is no more certain than is the prior philosophical assertion of God's reality. And God's reality, in this scenario, must be established by reason—unaided by revelation. Thus revelation becomes distinctly dependent on philosophy.

Third, all expositions of the "analogy of being" (the technical notion of partial correspondence between people and God) and all attempts to show the naturalness of theism—all "proofs" for God's existence and goodness, in other words—are logically loose. They state no more than possibilities (for probabilities are only one kind of possibilities) and can all be argued against indefinitely. This will damage the credit of any theology that appears to be building and relying on these arguments.

Fourth, the speculative method for building up a theology is inappropriate. As Louis Berkhof has observed, such a method takes humanity as its starting point and works from what it finds in humanity to what is found in God. "And in so far as it does this," Berkhof writes, "it makes man the measure of God." That, of course, does not "fit in a theology of revelation."

Fifth, there is always a risk that the foundations that natural theology lays will prove too narrow to build all the emphases of Scripture upon. For instance, in Thomas Aquinas's *Summa theologica* natural theology purports to establish that there is one God, who is the first cause of everything. But nothing is said about the personal aspects of God's being. This personal dimension is central to the biblical revelation of God, setting it in stark contrast with (for instance) the divine principle in Hindu thought. Aquinas's approach encourages the theologian to treat God as an impersonal object rather than a personal subject and to see himself or herself as standing over God to study him rather than under God to obey him.

It seems right to develop natural theology in the realm of supportive apologetics (showing biblical faith to be reasonable), but not to give it any place in our attempts to state what the biblical faith actually is.

Elements of mystification need to be purged. In retooling traditional theism for today we need to deal with a tendency toward mystification. By *mystification,* I mean the idea that some biblical statements about God mislead us and ought to be explained away.

To give an example, sometimes in Scripture God is said to change his mind and to make new decisions as he reacts to human doings. Orthodox theists have insisted that God did not really change his mind, since God is impassible and never a "victim" of his creation. As writes Louis Berkhof, representative of this view, "the change is not in God, but in man and man's relations to God." It is spoken of as a change in God because to us it looks as if it were.

But to say that is to say that some things that Scripture affirms about God do not mean what they seem to mean, and do mean what they do not seem to mean. That provokes the question, How can these statements be part of the revelation of God when they actually misrepresent and conceal God? So we have to ask ourselves how we may explain biblical statements about God's grief and repentance without seeming to explain them away.

Surely we must accept Barth's insistence that at every point in his self-disclosure, God reveals what he essentially is, with no gestures that mystify. And surely we must reject as intolerable any suggestion that God in reality is different at any point from what Scripture makes him appear to be. Scripture was not written to mystify, and therefore we need to ask how we can dispel the contrary impression that the time-honored, orthodox line of explanation leaves.

Three things seem to be called for as means to this end.

First, we need exegetical restraint in handling Scripture's anthropomorphisms (phrases using human figures to describe God). Anthropomorphism is characteristic of the entire biblical presentation of God. This is so, not because God bears humanity's image but because humans bear God's and hence are capable of understanding God's testimony to the reasons for his actions. The anthropomorphisms are there to show us why God acted as he did in the biblical story and how therefore he might act toward us in our own personal stories. But nothing that is said about God's negative or positive reactions to his creatures is meant to put us in a position where we can tell what it feels like to be God and determine, on this basis, what he can and cannot do. Our interpretation of the Bible must recognize this.

Second, we need to guard against a misunderstanding of God's changelessness. True to Scripture, this must not be understood as a beautiful pose, eternally frozen, but as the Creator's moral constancy, his unwavering faithfulness and dependability. God's changelessness is not a matter of intrinsic immobility but of moral consistency. God is always in action. He enters constantly into the lives of his creatures. There is change around him, change in people's relations to him and hence change in his treatment of them. But, to use the words of Louis Berkhof again, "there is no change in his being, his attributes, his purpose, his motives of action, or his promises." When one conceives of God's immutability in this biblical way, as a moral quality that is expressed whenever God changes his way of dealing with people for moral reasons, the biblical references to such change will cease to mystify.

Third, we also need to rethink God's impassibility. This conception of God represents no single biblical term but was introduced into Christian theology in the second century. What was it supposed to mean? The historical answer is not impassivity, unconcern and impersonal detachment in the face of the creation, nor inability or unwillingness to empathize with human pain and grief. It means simply, as we began to see earlier, that God's experiences do not come upon him as ours come upon us. His are foreknown, willed and chosen by himself and are not involuntary surprises forced on him from outside, apart from his own decision, in the way that ours regularly are.

Let us be clear: a totally impassive God would be a horror and not the God of Calvary at all. He might belong in Islam; he has no place in Christianity. If, therefore, we can learn to think of the *chosenness* of God's grief and pain as the essence of his impassibility, we will do well.

Elements of rationalism need to be purged. The final step needed to correct traditional theism is to purge it of invading streaks of rationalism. Just as the two-year-old son of a man with a brain like Einstein's could not understand all that was going on in his father's mind even if his father told him, so it is beyond us to understand all that goes on in the all-wise and not in any way time-bound mind of God.

But just as the genius who loves his child will take care to speak at the child's own level, even though that means reducing everything to baby talk, so does God when he opens his mind and heart to us in the Scriptures. The child, though aware that his father knows far more than he is currently saying, may yet learn from him all that he needs to know for a full and happy relationship with Dad. Similarly, Scripture, viewed as *torah* (God's fatherly law), tells us all that we need to know for faith and godliness.

We must never forget that we are in the little boy's position. At no point dare we imagine that the thoughts about God that Scripture teaches us take the full measure of his reality. The fact that God condescends and accommodates himself to us in his revelation certainly makes possible clarity and sureness of understanding. Just as certainly, however, it involves limitation in the revelation itself.

But we forget this, or so it seems, and then appears the rationalism of which I am speaking. It is more, I think, a temper than a tenet, but it produces a style of speech that, in effect, denies that there is anything about God we do not know. By thus failing to acknowledge God's incomprehensibility beyond the limits of what he has revealed, we shrink him in thought down to our size. The process is sometimes described as "putting God in a box."

It is certainly proper to stress, against the sleep of reason in the world and the zaniness of subjectivism in the church, that scriptural revelation is rational. But the most thoroughgoing Bible believers are sometimes required, like Job, to go on adoring God when we do not specifically understand what he is doing and why he is doing it.

We should avoid like the plague any talk that suggests we have enlisted God on our side and now have him in our pockets. Confidence in the teaching of God's written Word is to be maintained all the time. But this stance of theological triumphalism is something quite different and is to be avoided.

God the Image Maker

This review of traditional theism and suggestions for its possible refinement has been rough sledding. How can it all be pulled together? Can we focus our theism in a phrase? I think so. I welcome the suggestion that we should speak of God as the *Image Maker.*

This phrase binds together the main theistic thrusts that our secular world needs to face. Say "God," and you point to the infinite, eternal, self-existent, self-revealing Father, Son and Holy Spirit. Say "Maker," and you point to the fundamental relationship between God and us. He is the Creator; we are his creatures. Say "Image Maker," and you point to the basis and presupposition of our knowledge of God, namely, the fact that he made us like himself. Included in that image are rationality, relationality and the capacity for that righteousness that consists of receiving and responding to God's revelation. We are able to know God because we are thinking, feeling, relating, loving beings, just as he is himself. Whatever else the image of God includes, it certainly involves this much.

I am no prophet, nor a prophet's son, but it seems fairly clear to me that pressure on conservative theology is still building up from exponents of religious relativism and pluralism. This is so both within the church (where some think that the more theologies there are, the healthier as well as merrier we will be) and outside it.

I expect over the next few decades to see the quest for a synthesis of world religions gain impetus, with constant attempts to assimilate Christianity into other faiths. We may expect a generation of debate on the program of moving through and beyond syncretism to a nobler religion than any that has yet been seen. That notion, which has emerged more than once in liberal circles, looks like an idea whose time, humanly speaking, has come. Countering it, I predict, will be the next round in the church's unending task of defending and propagating the gospel. If this guess is right, we will be badly at a disadvantage if we have not taken pains to brush up our theism, since the question of theism—whether we are going to think about God the Christian way or some other way—will be at the heart of the debate. So I hope we will take time out to prepare ourselves along the lines suggested—just in case.

4

THE PERSON
OF CHRIST

HE LATE W. H. GRIFFITH THOMAS TITLED ONE OF HIS BOOKS
Christianity Is Christ. He was right; so it is.

To describe Christianity as a creed plus a code would be
more usual but would not go so deep. That Christianity involves both
a creed and a code is a truth that none should query, but it needs to be
made clear that Jesus Christ himself is central to both. Where basic
beliefs about Jesus are denied and Christian behavior as he taught it
is not practiced, Christianity does not exist, whatever may be claimed
to the contrary.

A Person to Know

But Thomas's point was that you can know the creed and embrace the
code and still be a stranger to Christianity, and as I said, he was right.
Martin Luther, George Whitefield and John Wesley, to name but three,
had to learn that through humbling experience. So did I, and so have
many more. The essence of Christianity is neither beliefs nor behavior
patterns. It is the reality of communion here and now with Christian-

ity's living founder, the Mediator, Jesus Christ.

Christianity proclaims that Jesus of Nazareth, the Galilean preacher, was a divine person, the incarnate Son of God. Christianity calls him "Christ" because that is his official title. It identifies him as the long-awaited Messiah, the divinely anointed Savior-King of all humanity. Christianity interprets the criminal's death that he suffered as fulfilling a divine purpose—the salvation of sinners. And Christianity affirms that after his death Jesus came alive again, in human flesh, mysteriously transformed, and has from that time been exercising full supremacy over the entire cosmic order.

Invisibly present to uphold us as we trust, love, honor and obey him, he supernaturalizes our natural existence, remaking our characters on the model of his own, constantly energizing us to serve and nurture others for his sake. When life ends, whether through the arrival of our own heart-stopping day or through his public reappearance to end history with judgment, he will take us to be with him. Then we shall see his face, share his life, do his will and praise his name with a joy that will exceed any ecstasy of which we are now capable and that will go on literally forever.

That is the gospel. It is indeed good news.

Being a Christian, therefore, is a matter of constantly reaching out to the invisibly present Savior by words and actions that express three things: The first is *faith* in him as the one who secured, and now bestows, forgiveness of our sins, so setting us right with the God who is his Father by essence and becomes ours by adoption. The second is *love* for him as the One who loved us enough to endure an unimaginably dreadful death in order to save us. The final thing expressed is *hope* in him as the sovereign Lord through whose grace our life here, with all its pains, is experienced as infinitely rich and our life hereafter will be experienced as infinitely richer.

It thus appears that Christianity is Christ *relationally*. Being a Christian is knowing Christ, which is more than just knowing about him. Real faith involves real fellowship. "Our fellowship," explained the apostle John, "is with the Father and with his Son, Jesus Christ" (1 Jn 1:3). Credence without this communion is only halfway to Christianity. Personal homage, trust and obedience are what finally count.

The Christian centuries have seen a vast company of believers who have shown that they understood this well, even when their official teachers were not stating it well. This knowledge of Christ sustained Christians in the catacombs and in the arena during 250 years of persecution before Constantine. This same knowledge upheld Protestant martyrs in Britain and Western Europe in the sixteenth century and the persecuted Puritans, Covenanters and Huguenots of the seventeenth. This knowledge has supported missionaries, who have been laying down their lives for Christ since the days of the Jesuit pioneers, and also countless thousands who have suffered for Christ in our time in Africa, Asia, China, the Middle East and the former Soviet Union.

What should we make, and what should we ask the world to make, of these heroic believers who remained so peaceful, patient and kind through all they endured? Their secret was an open one; it is really no secret at all. They embraced Paul's certainty that nothing can separate us from the love of God that is in Christ Jesus our Lord (Rom 8:38). They took to themselves Christ's words to the church at Smyrna: "Be faithful, even to the point of death, and I will give you the crown of life" (Rev 2:10). With these assurances they died, as they had lived, in joy and triumph. Their faith in and love for their divine Savior, and their readiness to exchange the present life for a better one at his call, are the authentic marks of Bible Christianity. This is the real thing.

Against the backdrop of this supernatural, faithful heroism that demonstrates so fully the credibility of the Christian faith, if you were told that many in the churches nowadays have come to minimize and even deny the deity and sole saviorhood of Jesus Christ, you might conclude that they were in a state of spiritual delirium of some kind.

And such, I believe, is the case. Sleeping sickness of the spirit, with people talking in their sleep, is my own diagnosis of this tragic state of affairs. Let me describe more exactly what I see.

For a century now, not just among outsiders but within Protestant bodies too, there has been a massive drift into a lowered view of Jesus as a good and godly man who is simply an inspiring example rather than an almighty Savior. This trend has produced great confusion and weakness. People nowadays do not know the truth about Jesus. Many of them, if they are in a church (which most of them are not), do not know what they are expected to believe about Christ. They see that the clergy are often confused on the subject, and they know many church people who hold views about Jesus that are quite different from what their church professes. What seems to be assumed by all is that to say anything more about Jesus than that he was a fine man is to enter the realm of speculation, where no norms for thought exist and no one has any right to impose his or her views on anyone else.

A sad scene? Yes, very. How did it come to be? By stages, thus.

From Whence It Came

Three centuries ago, Protestant intellectual culture—philosophical, scientific, literary and aesthetic—tugged loose from its historic moorings in the Christian faith. Brilliant thinkers shrank the idea of God smaller and smaller, distorting it in the process and distorting belief about Jesus with it. That is why today's average person has only out-of-shape notions about the Father and the Son, seen, as it were, through the wrong end of a telescope.

Specifically, the Reformers had proclaimed the sovereign Lord of scriptural faith, the God who speaks what the Bible says and who saves sinners through Christ by grace. But seventeenth-century deists ruled out miracles and set a fashion of denying that God is Lord over the world. Then in the eighteenth century the philosopher Kant made a fashion out of denying verbal revelation, and nineteenth-century thinkers went on to domesticate God as the power behind the universal evolutionary processes that they posited. Now our own era has settled for a finite, kindhearted, ineffective, suffering God, a sort of heavenly uncle whose goodwill makes no real difference to anything, a being who it is nice to think exists but who, ultimately, is not worth bothering about. You have met this rather pathetic figure: he is the God in whom the average North American today believes.

Thoughts about Jesus shrank similarly. Seventeenth-century skepticism about miracles made the incarnation an embarrassment, and eighteenth-century skepticism about revelation reduced the words of Jesus from divine disclosures to something far less. Since the nineteenth century, Jesus has been viewed as a supreme instance of human religious development, who probably did not rise from the dead and certainly does not rule the world at present, but whose memory still has influence, as does that of Socrates or Winston Churchill. This, however, does not affirm Jesus' continuing personal ministry but denies it. It says that he was not God incarnate but was a man whom God indwelt, and that he is important to us as a sample of sainthood rather than as a supernatural Savior from the guilt and power of sin.

Why It Continues

This was bad enough, but four further factors in world Protestantism have made it worse by ensuring that these views are persistently propagated at this time. First, the theological colleges and seminaries and, in Germany particularly, the theological faculties of universities that prepare each generation of clergy for their lifework, have largely surrendered to this skepticism about Christ. They teach it to their students, who naturally swallow it and then spread it in the churches where they serve.

Second, the so-called higher biblical criticism (which is no more than the necessary attempt to find out when, where, how, by whom and why each book of Scripture was written) has for more than a century been controlled by the antimiraculous assumptions about God of which we spoke above. As a result, it has come to be thought, quite wrongly, that scientific scholarship has shown the untrustworthiness of much of the Bible, including its delineation of Jesus as the supernatural Savior, and that any attitude of belief in the Bible and its Christ must hence be judged unscholarly.

Third, the practice of making children memorize catechisms or creeds stating Christian doctrine has fallen out of use. Modern Sunday schools mostly limit themselves to teaching Bible stories. Children thus grow up in the church without being drilled in its creed. They learn of Jesus as friend and helper, without ever hearing that he is the second person of the Trinity and so become adults to whom this fact is altogether strange.

Fourth, as the West's sense of human sinfulness has diminished and its awareness of other religions has intensified, the idea has taken root that Christianity is merely a mindset and behavior pattern that is seen in all good people, whatever faith or lack of faith they may profess. Along with this goes the sense that Christianity is acquired by instinct and osmosis rather than by instruction.

Since no one knows about Jesus without instruction, this view would seem to imply that Jesus himself is not essential to Christianity. That, I suspect, is what many believe deep down, though few are bold enough to say it aloud.

With all these factors as part of the scene, it is small wonder that great companies of churchgoers today think of God in a unitarian rather than trinitarian way, of Christ in terms of God-indwelt humanity rather than of incarnate deity and of salvation in terms of being accepted through God's forbearance for trying to do right rather than of being forgiven through Christ's atonement for actually doing wrong. But it is tragic that we who inherit so rich a legacy of true faith, past and present, should have gone so far astray on matters so fundamental. It shows, of course, that God has no grandchildren; grace and wisdom do not run in the blood. No doubt the devil laughs at our lapses, but I hope no one else does. They are too serious for that.

What it all amounts to is that in today's church, historic Christian belief in Jesus Christ is like Humpty Dumpty: it has had a great fall and now lies before us broken in pieces. Everyone picks up some of these, but few have them all or know what to do with those they have.

There is much genuine perplexity. Persons of goodwill who want to be Christians look to clergy and theologians for help, find them in disarray regarding the person and place of Jesus, and with some impatience and disgust, turn away from them to settle for their own private thoughts about the man from Galilee. Yet they know that these are no more than amateurish fancies and guesses, and they would be very glad if they could be given something surer and more definite.

What True Believers Can Do

For the sake of those who seek a wiser way, we ask with some urgency: Can Christian certainty about Jesus Christ be reconstructed? Can Humpty Dumpty be put together again? I think the answer is yes, and I now offer guidelines for doing this.

1. Link the person of Jesus with his work. All accounts of Jesus Christ really answer two questions: not just the question about his person (who he was and is), but also the one about his work (what he did and does). The first question is ontological, the second functional, and they are distinct. Nonetheless, they are also related, as one's answer to the second is likely to affect one's answer to the first.

If, under the influence of skepticism about the Bible, one should limit Jesus' work to instruction (teaching God's will) and demonstration (of God's love and of godliness) and play down his dominion (his present heavenly reign and future return to judge all people) and reduce communion with him to being moved by his example, then one will lose nothing by diminishing him to the status of a uniquely enlightened human being, a man who reflected God in an especially clear way. Such a nonsupernatural view of Jesus will seem simple, sufficient and appealing.

But for sober Christians who heed the apostles' understanding of Jesus and his own recorded understanding of himself as the sole mediator between God and ourselves, our substitutionary sin-bearer on the cross, our risen Redeemer here and now, and the one in whom and through whom we have eternal life, it is a very different story. Such Christians give full weight to the New Testament account of Christ's salvation as a matter of literal union and communion with him here and hereafter. They notice that the New Testament sees prayer and praise to Jesus as no less proper than praise and prayer to the Father. They discern that the New Testament actually hails Jesus as the living Lord who, alongside the Father, is personally divine, and they declare that in the New Testament, as in the Christian community since, personal fellowship with the risen Lord is a reality of experience.

Their conclusion is that to categorize Jesus as a God-indwelt man, now dead, is to fall grievously short, for such a Christ could not bring us the salvation that the New Testament proclaims.

Where the dimensions of salvation are diminished or obscured, there the New Testament account of Jesus' role as Redeemer is likely to be scaled down to match. What else would you expect? Here lies the explanation for most of the poor Christology that the world has seen in our time. But those who appreciate the greatness and the glory of Jesus' saving work will not lapse in this way.

2. Understand Jesus' identity in trinitarian terms. Our one God is a complex unity, to whose personal life oneness and threeness are equally basic. For this unique and unparalleled fact the New Testament has no technical terminology, and it took Christians three hundred years of debate before they learned to express and safeguard it by confessing one God in three persons and declaring the Son and Spirit to be one in essence with the Father.

But trinitarian thinking about God is found constantly throughout the New Testament, most strikingly so when Jesus explains that after his going to the Father "another counselor," the Holy Spirit, will be sent to replace him and that through the Spirit's coming he himself will come to the disciples in the present. They will then know that he lives in them and that they live in him (Jn 14:12-23; 16:5-28). Evidently, then, Jesus and the Spirit are somehow linked and on a par with each other, just as Jesus testified that he and his Father were. The truth of the Trinity is here coming into view.

The New Testament writers consistently see salvation as the joint work of Father, Son and Holy Spirit, the Father arranging it, the Son accomplishing and administering it, and the Holy Spirit applying it. Therefore, if one denies the Trinity, the truth about salvation will inevitably be lost also. It is thus basic to Christianity, as distinct from all other world religions, always to think about God in trinitarian terms.

Rather than loosely referring to Jesus as "God incarnate," as if unitarianism is true and "Jesus" is a second role that the eternal Father has played, we should always describe him as "Son of God incarnate." For it was precisely the second person of the eternal three, not the first or third, who took humanity to himself.

Among some New Testament scholars today it is fashionable to maintain that passages like John 1:1-14, Philippians 2:5-7, Colossians 1:15-17 and Hebrews 1—2 affirm that the Son existed before the incarnation only as a thought in the Father's mind, not as an eternal person distinct from the Father. Whether they see that this view denies the eternal Trinity I do not know, but it obviously does. It is so unnatural and forced as an interpretation, however, that we need not spend time discussing it here.

3. Do not soft-pedal Jesus' humanness. John's statement that the Word became flesh (Jn 1:14) means more than that he encased himself in a physical body. It means that he took to himself and entered right into everything that contributes to a fully human experience. From the moment he became a fetus in Mary's womb up to the present, human experience has been one dimension of the life of the Son of God. It will continue to be so forever.

By virtue of what he experienced as a healthy first-century Jewish male before his death at thirty-three, Jesus can now enter sympathetically into all human experiences, those of girls and women, sick folk, the aged and addicts (for instance) no less than those of young males like himself (see Heb 2:18; 4:15-16). This is amazing, but it is true. Thus he is able to give to all the help toward right living that we all need.

The church has always known this. That is why such ideas as that Jesus only appeared to be human but really was not, or that the incarnate Son had no human mind or will, have always been condemned as heresy. And that is why Christians have been constantly asking Jesus to help them in their struggles ever since the days of the apostles—and constantly testifying that he does.

For more than a hundred years it has been argued that we who believe that Jesus' humanness is "adjectival" (so to speak) to his deity cannot take his humanness seriously. We do indeed believe that the deepest secret of his identity is that he is "God plus," a divine person ontologically and experientially enlarged by his manhood, rather than being "man plus," a human person uniquely indwelt and enriched by his God. But that does not mean that his life was not as fully human as yours or mine.

It is certainly true that believers in the incarnation have often talked as if there were some experiences—the suffering of Calvary, for one—that Jesus went through "in his humanity" but not "in his deity." But that idea should be replaced by the thought that Jesus experienced everything in the unity of his divine-human person.

The true Christian claim at this point is that the incarnation made direct entry into human frustration and pain possible for the Son of

God, who then out of love actually entered in person into the agony of crucifixion and the greater agony of Godforsakenness (see Mk 15:34) in order to bear our sins and so redeem us. Never let this claim be played down.

4. Do not diminish Jesus' divinity. An unhappy speculation that has mesmerized many during the past century is the so-called kenosis theory, which suggests that in order to enter into a fully human experience of limitation, the Son of God at his incarnation forfeited his natural powers of omnipotence and omniscience. As a result, there were things that he wanted to do that he could not do and mistakes due to ignorance could not be kept out of his teaching. Four comments seem to be called for by way of reaction.

First, there is no hint of any such forfeiture in Scripture.

Second, the suggestion seems clearly to undermine Jesus' authority as a teacher and thus to dishonor him and create problems for us.

Third, it raises a perplexity about Jesus' present heavenly life. If Jesus' exercise of the two abilities mentioned (the Son's natural power to do and know whatever he willed to do and know) is incompatible with a fully human experience, it would seem to follow that if in heaven he resumed these powers, his heavenly experience is not now fully human, or else, if his heavenly experience remains fully human, he has not regained these powers and never will. I leave it to the proponents of the kenosis theory to struggle with this dilemma; it is not my problem, nor I hope yours.

Fourth, the natural explanation of the one bit of evidence from the Gospels cited in support of the theory—Jesus' acknowledged ignorance of the time of his return (Mk 13:32)—is that since the Son's nature is not to take initiatives (see Jn 5:19) but to follow his Father's prompting, his reason for not doing certain things or bringing to conscious knowledge certain facts was simply that he knew that his Father did not wish this done.

In other words, the times when Jesus was noticeably not exercising the powers of omniscience and omnipotence should be explained in terms not of the special conditions of the incarnation but of the inner life of the Trinity, in which it is the Son's nature to be led entirely by his Father's will.

To follow these paths of thought is, I believe, to avoid the pitfalls that in our day threaten incarnational thinking. Thus we can be led back out of confusion to regain a truly biblical faith in Jesus Christ. How much we today need to do this! Surely there will be no renewal of life and power from God in our churches until we learn again to see the glory of Jesus Christ, our incarnate Lord. May God teach us all this lesson—soon!

5

WHY THE
CROSS?

W E PREACH CHRIST CRUCIFIED," WROTE PAUL: "A STUM-
bling block to Jews and foolishness to Gentiles" (1 Cor
1:23). We can understand these reactions. The impact of
Paul's message was as if a modern American should announce his or
her everlasting allegiance to a person of dubious character as candidate
for the presidency who was actually sent to the electric chair. Yet Paul's
devotion and joy as he contemplates this grotesque-sounding phenomenon are total and absolute: "May I never boast," he says, "except
in the cross of our Lord Jesus Christ" (Gal 6:14). Why so? Because,
as he says elsewhere, "God demonstrates his own love for us in this:
While we were still sinners, Christ died for us" (Rom 5:8); "Christ
... loved me and gave himself for me" (Gal 2:20); "Christ redeemed
us from the curse of the law by becoming a curse for us" (Gal 3:13).
Now we are at the heart of the matter: the cross of Christ reveals the
love of God because it shows what that love is prepared to suffer for
the beloved.

I stand with Paul; let there be no misunderstanding about that. I believe, as he did, that the death of Christ exhibits the love of God richly, fully, glowingly and gloriously. I believe that Christ's death made atonement for my sins, just as Paul believed that it made atonement for his sins. And I believe, quite specifically, that the old-fashioned view of the cross as penal substitution under God's law gets us nearer to the heart of its meaning than any other picture that the New Testament contains. My reasons follow.

Understanding the Cross

The apostle Paul in Romans describes the work of the cross as follows:

> Now a righteousness from God, apart from law, has been made known, to which the Law and the Prophets testify. This righteousness from God comes through faith in Jesus Christ to all who believe. There is no difference, for all have sinned and fall short of the glory of God, and are justified freely by his grace through the redemption that came by Christ Jesus. God presented him as a sacrifice of atonement, through faith in his blood. He did this to demonstrate his justice, because in his forbearance he had left the sins committed beforehand unpunished— he did it to demonstrate his justice at the present time, so as to be just and the one who justifies those who have faith in Jesus. (Rom 3:21-26)

We see three things here immediately.

First, the atonement is a work of God. This paragraph comes at the conclusion of a long section (Rom 1:18—3:20) in which Paul has been dwelling on the condemnatory verdict of God as Judge of all humanity. His thought is crystallized when he says, "Because of your stubbornness and your unrepentant heart, you are storing up wrath against yourself for the day of God's wrath, when his righteous judgment will be revealed" (Rom 2:5). We notice the two phrases together: "day of God's wrath" and "righteous judgment . . . revealed." Wrath is not a fitful, petulant, childish, immoral thing in God. Wrath is the moral and judicial attribute expressed in righteous judgment. It is holiness rejecting sin.

At the end of this first great doctrinal section, Paul has reached the conclusion that the law of God exposes sin and guilt everywhere and brings all under condemnation. The whole world is held accountable to God, and by the works of the law (that is, by human activity at its best) no one will be justified in God's sight, for through the law comes knowledge of sin. This is a universal fact and the universal problem.

But now, Paul says, beginning a new subject, the righteousness of God is revealed in a different way from the way of judgment on wrongdoing. The phrase "righteousness from God" at the beginning of Romans 3:21 still means God's quality of doing right in everything he does; however, the issue of *this* display of God's righteousness is not our condemnation but its opposite: our justification. It sounds fantastic, too good to be true. But Paul goes on to explain that this is exactly what he means. This revelation of the righteousness of God is a disclosure of God in action, setting sinners right with himself, justifying them (to use the word that he introduces in v. 24). *Justifying* means acquitting them from the charges that are leveled against them and designating them to be accepted and treated henceforth as if they were sinless, though they are in fact imperfect and guilty still. How can this be—this miracle of pardon and peace for people who by absolute standards must be judged "wicked" (Rom 4:5)? "By his [God's] grace through the redemption that came by Christ Jesus," replies Paul, "God presented him as a sacrifice" (Rom 3:24-25), which is our next point.

Second, the atonement has the nature of sacrifice. Look again at Romans 3:25. It tells us that God set forth his Son "as a sacrifice of atonement, through faith in his blood." *Blood* is New Testament shorthand, pointing to animal sacrifice as the type of the sacrificial death Christ died. *Blood* tells us that sacrifice is the clue we need for interpreting the nature of the atonement.

What does the sight of blood do to you? Some people find that it turns their stomachs and makes them feel quite faint. If you are one of those, you would have had a hard time in temple and tabernacle worship in ancient Israel, for much blood was spilled in the course of worship. Among the sacrifices offered to God were cereal offerings (the meal offerings) and liquid offerings (the drink offerings). But most of the offerings were of animals that were ceremonially slaughtered.

The worshiper would draw near with his perfect victim. He would lay his hand on the animal's head and kill it. The priest would then draw and collect the blood and pour it out on one of the altars of God, ordinarily the altar of burnt offering, though on the Day of Atonement blood had to be poured out on the altar of incense too (Ex 30:9-10). Thus was sacrifice made. It was specifically stated in the Old Testament rituals recorded in the early chapters of Leviticus that sin offerings and guilt offerings must take this form: an animal killed, and the blood drained and then thrown out at the base of the altars, as prescribed.

Romans 3:25 is not the only place where Paul speaks of Christ's death in this sacrificial terminology. In Romans 5:9 he says, "We have now been justified by his blood." In Ephesians 1:7 he says, "In him we have redemption through his blood." In Colossians 1:20, speaking of reconciliation (which is what *atonement* really means), he says that the Lord Jesus Christ made peace "through his blood, shed on the cross." Each time the word *blood* occurs, it is theological shorthand expressing the thought of sacrifice for sin.

Other New Testament writers speak of the blood of Christ in just the same way. Hebrews does so in more places than we can mention here—Hebrews 9:11-14, which will be quoted shortly, is just one example. First Peter 1:19 reminds us that we were redeemed by "the precious blood of Christ, a lamb without blemish or defect." First John 1:7 tells us that "the blood of Jesus, his [God's] Son, purifies us from all sin." As a literal idea, of course, this imagery makes our imagination boggle. Red blood not staining but purging and cleansing! But the theological meaning is right; Christ's blood, that is, his atoning sacrifice, does cleanse us from sin. Again, in Revelation the blood of Christ is referred to with the same sacrificial significance: "To him who loves us and has freed us from our sins by his blood . . . —to him be glory and power for ever and ever!" (1:5); "You are worthy to take the scroll and to open its seals, because you were slain, and with your blood you purchased men for God" (5:9). In all these texts the atonement of Christ is portrayed as having the nature of sacrifice.

Third, the atonement displays God's righteousness. Righteousness is that quality in God whereby he always does what is right, the quality whereby he maintains and meets the claims of the past in the present, giving to every man and woman what he owes them. That was Aristotle's definition of righteousness, and it is the fundamental biblical view of the righteousness of God also. God keeps his word; God fulfills his undertakings; God gives us our due.

This makes the righteousness of God in judgment very easy to understand, but it makes the righteousness of God in justifying sinners appear at first inexplicable because it sounds wrong. It is marvelous good news. But surely, we say, it is not right that God, the just Judge, should justify the ungodly, as Paul actually says he does in Romans 4:5. Can it be right for God to behave this way? That is the question to which Paul is addressing himself in the compressed words of Romans 3:25-26. He is telling us here that it really is right. It has become right, for God himself has made it so. It has become the only right thing for God to do in virtue of his having sent his Son to the cross to be our sin-bearer.

This aspect of righteousness, whereby claims are met, was described in Roman law as *satisfaction (satisfactio),* which means "doing enough *[satis facere]* to meet the claims that are there." Paul is saying that God justifies us in a way that fully meets the claims that are there.

Since the time of the great Anselm in the eleventh century, the

Christian church has rejoiced to use this word *satisfaction* as a term expressing the real significance of the sacrifice of Christ. As Anselm expounded satisfaction, it was a matter of restoring God's violated honor, and that indeed is part of the truth. But when Luther came along, half a millenium later, he broadened the idea of satisfaction by the light of the Bible and made the right and true point that the way Jesus Christ restores God's glory is through his enduring the penal retribution for sin that God himself had announced. The suffering of Christ glorifies God the Father and wins salvation for the sinner by being a satisfaction to God's justice. That is the thought Paul is expressing in Romans 3:25-26.

Paul tells us that God set forth his Son to be "a sacrifice of atonement" by his blood. Actually, the NIV margin more accurately renders Paul's word: "as the one who would turn aside his wrath, taking away sin." That is what the KJV meant by translating it as "propitiation." This, says Paul, was "to demonstrate his justice, because in his forbearance he had left the sins committed beforehand unpunished" (v. 25). He had indeed justified sinners. He had been doing it throughout the whole Old Testament period. But he had been doing it on no more substantial a basis than the offering of animal sacrifice. Anyone who thought about things might well have asked, "How can the death of an animal put away the sin of a human being?" There was no answer to that question once it was raised. So, right up to the death of the Lord Jesus, this great question mark hung over God's grace in forgiving sins.

People praised God for the reality of the mercy, but they could not see its basis in righteousness. "Now you can see it," says Paul. "Now God has made it plain." The redemption that is in Christ Jesus covered "the sins committed beforehand." It had retrospective efficacy, just as it has efficacy in the present and for the future also. So now Paul is able to say, "He did it to demonstrate his justice at the present time, so as to be just and the one who justifies those who have faith in Jesus"

(v. 26). Just justification—righteous remission of our sins and assured acceptance of our persons—is the consequence of the cross.

In other words, through the redemption that is in Christ Jesus, justice is done. Sin is punished as it deserves. But it is punished in the person of a substitute. Now we can see how it is that God's justification is just. Now we can see how God's justification of sinners is itself justified. God has shown his righteousness. The Father has satisfied himself, providing through his beloved Son the satisfaction that was due to the divine holiness. And so men and women may go free. "God propitiated himself," we may say. God both gave and received satisfaction through the death of Jesus Christ.

This is why the word *satisfaction* has been a precious word to the people of God down the centuries, as it is, for instance, in the consecration prayer of the Communion service in the prayer book of my own Anglican church: "Almighty God, our heavenly Father, who of thy tender mercy didst give thine only Son Jesus Christ to die upon the cross for our salvation, who made there, by his one oblation of himself once offered, a full, perfect and sufficient sacrifice, oblation and satisfaction for the sins of the whole world . . ." The Heidelberg Catechism also celebrates the reality of satisfaction as the focus of true faith in Christ: "My only comfort in life and death is that I belong to my faithful Saviour Jesus Christ, who with his precious blood has fully satisfied for all my sins." The word is rarely heard today, but I think that if we understood the atonement better, we would use it more.

Paul's presentation of the realities of sacrifice and satisfaction has given us a basic line of thought regarding the atonement, which we must now explore a little further.

Old Testament Rituals

Scholars dispute among themselves whether the deepest thought in the sacrificial rituals that God gave to his people in Old Testament times is of (1) a gift to God, (2) communion with God, or (3) the making of atonement before God. All three thoughts are certainly there. When the burnt offering was given to God and the whole carcass was consumed, clearly the thought of gift was present. Again, when in the making of the peace offerings a meal took place in the sanctuary, clearly the thought of communion with God was present. But I do not think there can be any doubt that the deepest and most fundamental thought was that of atonement.

In explaining the sacrificial system to his people in Old Testament times, God made this very plain. In Leviticus 17:11 we find him saying as the explanation of a prohibition that he has just given against the eating of blood: "The life of a creature is in the blood, and I have given it to you to make atonement for yourselves on the altar; it is the blood that makes atonement for one's life." The central thought is that where sin has taken place, death must follow. "The soul who sins is the one who will die" (Ezek 18:4) is the basic form of that principle. In the sacrificial system, however, we see God enacting an adjustment of it: the Israelite soul has sinned but the animal dies instead.

Some scholars have taken this to mean that the blood makes atonement for sin by somehow releasing a life force that reanimates and reenergizes the sinner's relationship with God, which sin has broken. That, however, is pure fancy; there is no evidence to back up such an idea. Every scriptural analogy and the attitude toward animal sacrifices throughout the Old Testament shows that the shedding of blood means the pouring out and terminating of life. The shed blood is a witness to the animal's death. It is to exhibit death that the blood is presented at the altar. This alone is the basis on which God promised forgiveness of sin to his Old Testament people when they transgressed. Bloodshedding in sacrifice, which means the laying down of life in death, is what atones.

Substitution

The essence of atoning sacrifice, as we now see, is the surrendering of life in substitution for the guilty, death-deserving party. This is the key reality, the heart of what was going on in the sacrificial ritual and the heart of what was going on when our Lord Jesus Christ died on Calvary two millennia ago.

Substitution is a word the church has learned to love. True, it does not occur in the Bible any more than *satisfaction* does, but it is used and cherished because it is the word that fits. It is the word that describes the essence of this sacrificial transaction. Think of the ritual of those Old Testament sacrifices and you will see this plainly. As we saw earlier, the sinner comes with his sacrifice, and what does he do? He puts his hand on the animal's head and then kills it. Could any action make more plain that this is a substitutionary death, that the animal is dying on behalf of its owner? This has been denied, but it is really too plain for us to doubt it.

The annual ritual of the scapegoat taught this same lesson even more vividly. This was a ritual of the Day of Atonement, when comprehensive propitiation was made for all the sins of the people during the previous year. The procedure is laid out for us in Leviticus 16. In this ritual the high priest, having first offered a sin offering to make atonement for himself, takes two goats, puts his hands on the head of one of them, and proceeds to "confess over it all the wickedness and rebellion of the Israelites—all their sins—and put them on the goat's head. He shall send the goat away into the desert in the care of a man appointed for the task. The goat will carry on itself all their sins to a solitary place; and the man shall release it in the desert" (Lev 16:21-22). What is the meaning of this ritual? It is not a propitiation in itself but a picture of propitiation—a picture, that is, of what happens when the sacrificial animal is killed and the blood is poured out at the base of the altar as a sign that a life has been taken. The scapegoat is a picture of the removing of sin.

This is made plain by what happens to the second goat. The second goat is the one that really counts. The action with the scapegoat shows what happens through the second goat, which is killed and offered as a sin offering in the normal way. The banishing of the scapegoat into the wilderness was an illustrative device to make plain to God's people that their sin had truly been taken away.

When the writer to the Hebrews speaks of Christ achieving what the Day of Atonement typified, that is, our perfect and permanent cleansing from sin, he focuses not on the goat that went away into the wilderness but on the animal that was offered in sacrifice once a year by the high priest.

> When Christ came as high priest of the good things that are already here, he went through the greater and more perfect tabernacle that is not man-made, that is to say, not a part of this creation. He did not enter by means of the blood of goats and calves; but he entered the Most Holy Place once for all by his own blood, having obtained eternal redemption. The blood of goats and bulls and the ashes of a heifer sprinkled on those who are ceremonially unclean sanctify them so that they are outwardly clean. How much more, then, will the blood of Christ, who through the eternal Spirit offered himself unblemished to God, cleanse our consciences from acts that lead to death, so that we may serve the living God! (Heb 9:11-14)

There is the blood of Christ fulfilling the whole pattern of the ritual of the Day of Atonement.

Do we need further confirmation of this? If we do, we can find it in Isaiah 53. In verse 10 it is stated explicitly that God is making his servant's life an offering for sin. In verses 4-6 we are told what that means: "we considered him stricken by God, smitten by him, and afflicted." Yes, but "he was pierced for *our transgressions,* he was crushed for *our iniquities;* the punishment that brought us peace was upon him, and by his wounds we are healed. We all, like sheep, have gone astray, each of us has turned to his own way; and the LORD has laid on him *the iniquity of us all"* (emphasis added). This is substitution.

In Paul's many assertions about the atonement I trace a certain conceptual hierarchy. Paul says, as we saw, "May I never boast except in the cross of our Lord Jesus Christ" (Gal 6:14). We might ask Paul, "Why do you thus glory and rejoice in Jesus' shameful execution?" Paul would reply, "Because the cross was a sacrifice, putting away sin, and that sacrifice brought redemption. It brought redemption, that is, purchase and deliverance out of suffering and bondage, because it achieved reconciliation, the restoring of relations of peace with God; and it achieved reconciliation because it made propitiation (by his death Christ has quenched God's wrath, so making peace), and it was a work of propitiation because it was a work of substitution under judgment. Only so could it cover sin, quench wrath, make peace and set us free from the penal bondage and eternal jeopardy that faced us otherwise."

Paul in other places in his writings makes substitution the essence of his explanation of the cross. For instance, in a passage quoted earlier, Galatians 3:13, Paul writes, "Christ redeemed us from the curse of the law [the expression of the holiness of God in threatened judgment]." And how did he do it? That is what the next clause tells us. Only the NIV translates it as it ought to be translated: "Christ redeemed us from the curse of the law *by becoming a curse for us* . . . that the blessing given to Abraham might come to the Gentiles through Christ Jesus" (v. 14, emphasis added). The blessing of Abraham is the gift of righteousness, as Paul has already said (v. 6). Christ redeemed us from the curse of the law by becoming that curse in our place, so that we sinners might be pardoned and set right with God.

Martin Luther got this message and spelled it out in his commentary on Galatians as vividly as it has ever been spelled out by anyone. He comments thus on Galatians 3:13: "All the prophets foresaw in spirit that Christ should become the greatest transgressor, murderer, adulterer, thief, rebel, blasphemer, and so on, that ever was or could be in all the world. For he, being made a sacrifice for the sins of the whole world, is not now an innocent person and without sins . . . but a sinner."

Luther is, of course, talking about the imputing of our wrongdoing to Christ as our substitute. He continues,

> Our most merciful Father . . . sent his only Son into the world and laid upon him . . . the sins of all men, saying: You be Peter that denier; Paul that persecutor, blasphemer, and cruel oppressor; David that adulterer; that sinner who ate the apple in Paradise; that thief who hung on the cross; in short, you be the person who has committed all the sins of everyone; see therefore that you pay and satisfy for them. Here now comes the law [God, in his character as assessor and judge] and says: I find him a sinner . . . therefore let him die upon the cross. And so it sets upon him and kills him. By this means the whole world is purged and cleansed from all sins.

Luther understood substitution!

Colossians 2:14 is another glowing verse, full of imagery, in which Paul explains how he can assert so confidently that God has forgiven us all our trespasses. This is how he has done it, says Paul: "Having canceled the written code, with its regulations, that was against us and that stood opposed to us; he took it away, nailing it to the cross." Think that one out. The written code is, as it were, the IOU by which God binds us. It is nothing other than the requirement of his law, which we are bound to meet under pain of damnation. Anyone who fails to settle the IOU is in trouble, and that is the trouble we were all in. We owed God perfect obedience to his law, but we failed to obey the law, and so the IOU had become our death warrant. We stood under the curse of the law, there and nowhere else. But now, says Paul, God has canceled the legal bond "that stood opposed to us; he took it away, nailing it to the cross" (v. 14).

Look at the cross with the eye of faith, says Paul, and you will see that the superscription of the Savior's accusation does not read, "This is the king of the Jews." Oh, the eye of sense will see that, for that is what Pilate wrote, as all four Gospels record. But the eye of faith sees a different charge written up there. The stated cause of sentence and execution that the eye of faith sees is the long list of our own stumbles and shortcomings, as measured by the bond that was our spiritual death warrant. This shows us why Christ was there, hanging on the cross and enduring the truly hellish experience of Godforsakenness. He was the substitute for us, paying the penalty incurred by our moral failure and disobedience.

In Colossians 2:15 Paul goes on to tell us more of what we should be seeing as in faith we gaze at Calvary. We should realize, he says, that on the cross Christ "disarmed the powers and authorities." This means that he shook them off him, as one shakes off a garment that one is discarding; or perhaps the nuance is that he demoted and disgraced them. Furthermore, Paul says, Christ "made a public spectacle of them, triumphing over them by the cross." The principalities and powers, Satan and his hosts, were concerned at all costs to see that Jesus' venture of putting away our sin should fail. They tempted him to abandon the way of the cross (see Mt 4:5-10; 16:23; 26:37-44) and assaulted him in ways beyond our imagining as he endured the cross. But on the cross Jesus defeated them for all time.

Looking at the cross with the eye of sense, you might think you were looking at a wretched failure—a good man being lost to the world as the result of a miscarriage of justice. You might see it as a shocking scandal, a sad end to his ministry and a total tragedy. But look at the cross with the eye of faith, says Paul, and what you see is victory. You see the Savior triumphing over his enemies and so guaranteeing our final deliverance from Satan's sway. *Triumphing* has a precise meaning: it signifies leading in captivity, as a Roman general would lead enslaved captives in procession through Rome itself after a successful campaign. In and by his enduring of our punishment, Jesus showed that his and our spiritual foes are now powerless against him. Penal substitution thus brought personal victory.

Now look at what Paul says in 2 Corinthians 5:21: "God made him who had no sin to be sin for us [not by committing sin but by having our sins reckoned to his account], so that in him we might become the righteousness of God." He has just said that God in Christ was reconciling the world to himself (v. 19). How so? we ask. Answer: by not imputing our trespasses to us. And how is it that he does not do that? It is by virtue of the fact that he imputes them to the Lord Jesus so that Jesus pays for them in our stead. Substitution bringing about justification (righteousness before God): that is the message of this verse!

In our writing and preaching we cast around for illustrations of this, and it is good that we do. None are perfect, but they help. For instance, there is the story of Shamil, the Tartar general, who found that some member of his army was leaking secrets to the enemy and who threatened many lashes with the whip once the culprit was discovered. Shamil had been taking his whole household with him on his campaign, and it turned out that it was his own mother who had been leaking the secrets. Shamil shut himself up in his tent. Nobody saw him for two days. Then someone ventured to make his way into the tent to see what was going on. He found Shamil lashing himself.

Again, we tell the story of the Scottish soldier recorded by Ernest Gordon in the book *Through the Valley of the Kwai.* Gordon narrates the nightmarish business in World War II in which prisoners were used to build a Japanese military railroad through southeast Asia across the river Kwai. The shovels, says Gordon, were counted at the end of the day's work. On one occasion the Japanese guard reckoned that there was one short and that this must mean that some member of the work party had stolen his shovel and traded it to the Thais. Nobody admitted to doing this. The guard became furious and started yelling, "All die! All die!" He actually raised his rifle and pointed it at random at the men in the line. A soldier then stepped forward and said, "I did it." The guard went up to him, raised his rifle and beat the man's head in so that he died. When they got the shovels back to the camp, they were counted again and there was no shovel missing. The first count had been inaccurate. A man had given his life for his fellows.

Such stories get us some way along the road of illustrating the reality of the substitution that the New Testament spells out in these passages at which we have been looking.

God So Loved

Luther gazed at Christ's cross with steady joy and gloried in the fact that whoever trusts Christ can be assured of his love. He once wrote to a troubled friend, "Learn to know Christ and him crucified. Learn to sing to him, and say, 'Lord Jesus, you are my righteousness, I am your sin. You have taken upon yourself what is mine and given me what is yours. You have become what you were not so that I might become what I was not.' " There has been an exchange, a great and wonderful exchange (Luther actually used that phrase, a "wonderful exchange"), whereby the Son of God has taken all our guilt in order to set upon us all his righteousness. Was there ever such love?

Rabbi Duncan was a great old Reformed teacher in New College, Edinburgh, a hundred and more years ago. In one of his famous excursions in his classes, where he would move off from the Hebrew he was supposed to be teaching to theological reflections on this or that, he threw out the following question: "Do you know what Calvary was? What? What? What? Do you know what Calvary was?" Then, having waited a little and having walked up and down in front of them in silence, he looked at them again and said, "I'll tell you what Calvary was. It was damnation, and he took it lovingly." The students in his class reported that there were tears on his face as he said this. And well there might be. "Damnation, and he took it lovingly." Amazing love indeed!

Calvin's exposition of the clause of the creed that says "He descended into hell" related it to the three hours of darkness on the cross, when the Son felt himself forsaken of his Father because he was bearing the world's sin. Probably that is not what the creed originally meant, but it is a correct exposition of the truth about the cross. What love!

Deep, rich and full peace of conscience comes only when you know that your sins have been not simply disregarded but judged, judged to the full and paid for in full by the Son of God in your place. This is expressed in a beautiful hymn by Augustus M. Toplady, a hymn to which he gave the title "Faith Reviving." This is the troubled Christian finding peace again.

From whence this fear and unbelief?
Has not the Father put to grief
His spotless Son for me?
And will the righteous Judge of men
Condemn me for that load of sin
Which, Lord, was charged on thee?

Complete atonement thou hast made
And to the utmost farthing paid
Whate'er thy people owed.
Nor can God's wrath on me take place
When sheltered 'neath thy righteousness
And covered by thy blood.
If thou my pardon hast secured
And freely in my room endured
The whole of wrath divine,
Payment God cannot twice demand,
First from my bleeding surety's hand
And then again from mine.

Return, my soul, unto thy rest;
The sorrows of thy great High Priest
Have bought thy liberty.
Trust in his efficacious blood,
Nor fear thy banishment from God
Since Jesus died for thee.

If you want to know what it means to say that Christ died for someone, for you or for me, that hymn tells you. If ever you asked, "Why the cross?"—well, now you know.

Now you can see why Richard Hooker, that great Anglican theologian of the sixteenth century, wrote this at the end of his *Learned Sermon on Justification:* "Let men count it folly, or frenzy, or whatsoever. We care for no knowledge, no wisdom in the world but this, that man has sinned and God has suffered, that God has been made the sin of man, and man is made the righteousness of God." My sin has been judged already, its penalty fully paid. "Payment God cannot twice demand, first from my bleeding surety's hand and then again from mine." I am forgiven and accepted in Jesus, the beloved Son of God.

Folly? Frenzy? No. Simply grace and mercy. That is my peace; I trust it is yours. Here is the place of joy and glory, of thanksgiving, of the almost overwhelming delight to which scriptural meditations on Christ's death as sacrifice, substitution and satisfaction lead us. "Thanks be to God for his indescribable gift!" (2 Cor 9:15).

6

THE HOLY SPIRIT
& CHRISTIAN
GROWTH

THE CHRISTIAN LIFE BEGINS WITH NEW BIRTH, AND BIRTH IS meant to issue in growth. In the New Testament, spiritual growth is a *fact*, and it is described as growth in faith and love for others. For instance, at the beginning of 2 Thessalonians Paul praises God for the way in which the Thessalonian believers had grown: "We ought always to thank God for you, brothers, . . . because your faith is growing more and more, and the love every one of you has for each other is increasing" (2 Thess 1:3).

We find further that growth in grace is a *goal* for which the apostles prayed and to which they gave direction. Thus Paul, in 1 Thessalonians 3:12, had prayed exactly for that for which he was praising God at the beginning of the second letter. He prayed, "May the Lord make your love increase and overflow for each other and for everyone else." He prayed that they might increase in love, and he was seeing the answer to his prayers when he later praised God that they were increasing in love. Colossians (1:10-12) and Philippians (1:9-11) show Paul praying that believers might grow in faith and love and abound in good works. Peter gave directions for growth at the beginning of his first letter, saying, "Like newborn babies, crave pure spiritual milk [that is, the Word of God], so that by it you may grow up in your salvation" (1 Pet 2:2).

"Grow . . . in grace!" implores Peter (2 Pet 3:18). To grow in grace is not an option but an order. You know what joy it is to parents to have a baby, but just imagine if the months and years went by and their baby never grew. Imagine that at the end of five or ten years their baby was still twenty inches long, lying helpless in a crib, not having grown. No one would be rejoicing then. It would be a horrible tragedy. And it is equally horrible when the children of God, newborn babes in Christ, fail to grow toward the stature of their Savior. As Arthur Pink once said, "It brings no glory to God that his children should be dwarfs."

Foundations of Growth

I have four things to touch on in trying to spell out the meaning of spiritual growth: its *foundations,* some *mistakes* about it, its *dimensions* and its *means.*

First, we will look at the foundations of growth. Three facts constitute the basis for it. Fact number one is *regeneration by grace through the Holy Spirit,* the event that Paul in Titus 3:5 calls "rebirth and renewal by the Holy Spirit." When people turn to God, we call it conversion. But we know that God works in people to make them will and act for his good pleasure, and it is only because he so works that we turn to God. Thus our turning to God in repentance and faith is equally God turning us to himself by the sovereign work and power of his Holy Spirit. When we think of this great change as our turning to God, we call it conversion, as was said above; but when we think of it as God turning us to himself, we call it regeneration or new birth. Conversion and regeneration are thus the same change of direction, viewed from two different angles.

Not all theologians have said it quite like that. Moderns often identify regeneration with the moment of God's enlivening of the personal core of our being (our heart, as Scripture calls it), and view the conversion process as the fruit of this act of creation. John Owen, the Puritan who of all English-speaking theologians seems to me the greatest, would not have queried the substance of this. Indeed, he insisted on it himself when he talked about effectual calling. But he thought it more scriptural to correlate regeneration and conversion as two aspects of the same reality. He presents conversion as my action, psychologically speaking, but equally and fundamentally as God's work in me, for which God must have all the praise and glory. I have a mild preference for Owen's usage and will adhere to it in what follows.

God's work of regeneration, then, the work of which conversion is the psychological form, is the first foundation of growth in grace. Through regeneration we become new creatures, indwelt by the divine Holy Spirit, who wrought this great change in us in the first place. Growth in grace means going on from there; it is the living out, maturing and ripening of what God did within us when he turned us to himself.

Alongside this first foundation stands a second: *justification by grace through the Holy Spirit.* Regeneration and justification, that is, our pardon and acceptance by God, are two realities that go together. The passage from which I took the phrase "rebirth and renewal by the Holy Spirit" is really on justification. It begins in Titus 3:4 and reads thus:

> When the kindness and love of God our Savior appeared, he saved us, not because of righteous things we had done [there were no such deeds], but because of his mercy. He saved us through the washing [that consists] of rebirth and renewal by the Holy Spirit, whom he poured out on us generously through Jesus Christ our Savior, so that, having

been justified by his grace, we might become heirs having the hope of eternal life. This is a trustworthy saying. (vv. 4-8)

You see the links here: With new birth goes justification. The Spirit induces faith in Jesus Christ, faith brings justification (acquittal and acceptance by God in his character as judge), and with justification goes adoption into God's family and our instatement as God's heirs. Now we are God's children. His law is now our family code and no longer an oppressive burden as it was before we were converted. We see the law as an expression of our Father's will, and we delight to keep it because we want to please the One who loved us and saved us. Thus it is for all who are justified, and growth in grace is growth into this glad obedience.

The third fact, which goes with the first two, is *incorporation into Christ through the Holy Spirit.* As Paul says in Galatians 3:27, "All of you who were baptized into Christ have clothed yourselves with Christ." Now we are in Christ, sharing his risen life, united to him for time and eternity. Again Paul says in 1 Corinthians 12:13, "We were all baptized by one Spirit into one body [the body of Christ, which is the fellowship of all believing people]." Now, therefore, we are members of Christ's body in the basic scriptural sense of being his limbs, for that is what *members* means in the New Testament: limbs, organs, units, parts in the body of Christ. The head, Christ himself, animates and nourishes the whole so that the body, as Paul said in Ephesians 4:16, "grows and builds itself up in love." Our growth in grace is growth within the overall growth of the body. Christians ordinarily grow in fellowship, not apart from it.

Our individual growth in grace, which rests upon these three things, is that work of God in our lives that is pictured in 2 Corinthians 3:18—our being changed from glory to glory by the Lord who is the Spirit. We call it sanctification, but growth in grace is an equally proper name for it. This is the "good work" that Paul says he trusts God to complete in the lives of those in whom he has begun it (Phil 1:6). From another standpoint it is the work of God bringing forth in us what Galatians 5:22 calls "the fruit of the Spirit," namely, "love, joy, peace, patience, kindness, goodness, faithfulness, gentleness and self-control." As we look at those qualities, we realize that they are, quite simply, a profile of our Lord Jesus Christ, now to be reproduced in the lives of his followers. Growing in grace means that this reflection of the Savior's lovely and glorious moral character becomes more and more what we are in our character, attitudes and conduct.

Common Mistakes About Growth

God's people sometimes make mistakes when thinking about spiritual growth, and such mistakes can be a source of real trouble. Here are three.

Mistake number one is *to suppose that growth in grace is measurable* in the way that physical growth is measurable. My son, when he was growing up, liked from time to time to stand against the post of one of the doors in our home, level a pencil across the top of his head and mark his height there. The post came to bear a series of different marks, each dated, showing how he had been growing over the years. That is how it is in our physical lives. But what we are talking about here is a work of God that centers in our hearts at a level deeper than consciousness will take us. There is a divine mystery in the work by which God makes us grow in grace. We cannot measure it by any simple, regular assessment technique like measuring height or checking weight. What Scripture shows is that growth in grace is known by the way we behave under pressure, when times of testing and temptation come, when the heat is on and there is a crisis. Then our reaction and behavior will show whether we have been growing in grace or not.

A great example of this is Abraham. At the age of seventy-five he was promised a son. He and his wife were childless, but God undertook to give him an heir. He has waited eleven years and now is eighty-six, and his wife is only a few years younger. They think they cannot wait any longer. Their faith cracks. Sarah says to Abram (his name has not been changed to Abraham as yet), "Look, I shall never have a child. You have a son by Hagar, my maid, and then that child will count as ours, and thus the promised heir will appear." Thus Abram and Sarah conspired together to play amateur providence and bring God's promise to pass by unhallowed means. And they did it! Ishmael was born. But God never accepted Ishmael as Abram's heir. What Abram and Sarah did was a sad mistake, a testimony to immaturity in the life of faith (Gen 16).

But follow the story. God has renewed his promise of a son and changed Abram's name to Abraham (Gen 17). Isaac has actually arrived, born to a father who was about one hundred years old at the time. Now Isaac is a teenager, and Abram is a very elderly man indeed. At this point we read in Genesis 22: "God tested Abraham. He said to him, 'Abraham! . . . Take your son, your only son, Isaac, whom you love, and go to the region of Moriah. Sacrifice him there as a burnt offering' " (vv. 1-2). Do you suppose that any father's heart ever hurt more than Abraham's as he tramped up the mountain with Isaac? Do you suppose that any servant of God has ever been more strongly tempted to cry out, "This word from God is mad"? Hardly! But Abraham's faith had grown over the years, and this time he trusted God to know what he was doing. He was prepared at God's command to endure even the death of his son. This is the behavior of a man who has ripened in grace. It is our behavior under pressure that shows whether we have been growing in grace or not.

I remember talking to a clergyman friend who only two days before had been harassed by a woman in a counseling appointment. She had tried to seduce him, and he was still literally shaking as he thought of it. He had resisted, as Joseph long ago had resisted Potiphar's wife (Gen 39). But it was a shattering temptation, a real trauma for him. That is a further example of what I mean when I speak of crisis times, sudden testings, that show whether we have gotten our roots well down into the grace of God or not. Just as the impact of high winds shows whether trees have a good root system or not, so the times of testing show whether we have a spiritual root system anchored firmly in our Lord Jesus Christ.

Let us not make any mistake here. Though growth in grace cannot be measured by any simple process of assessment, it will be tested, as sure as eggs are eggs. As I conduct examinations to see what the members of my classes have learned, so God appoints testing times for us to see to what strength of mind and heart we have grown. It is for us to seek to walk with God in a way that guarantees that when the temptation comes it will find us rooted firmly in him. Then we will find with the temptation "a way out" (1 Cor 10:13), just as Abraham, in fact, found that he was not required to kill Isaac after all.

Mistake number two is *to suppose that growth in grace is a uniform process.* It is not so. There are growing times, when a person grows in the Lord much more rapidly than at other times. God, who finds us all different from each other when his grace first touches us, deals with different Christians in different ways.

Let me illustrate this from Scripture. Consider Peter. When Jesus called him, Peter was a hearty, warm-hearted, open-handed leadership type, as we would say. But he had one area of weakness. He was impulsive, headstrong and unstable. He suffered from what is sometimes called "foot-in-mouth disease." We frequently find him saying foolish things that he had not thought out and then not standing by them. On the evening of Jesus' betrayal he said to the Lord, "Even if all fall away on account of you, I never will" (Mt 26:33). But within a few hours of saying that, he was thrown into a panic by a servant girl's questions and denied his master three times. That was the blackest moment of Peter's pilgrimage. He went out, Luke says, and wept bitterly (Lk 22:62).

But now the crucified Jesus rises, ascends to heaven and pours out the Spirit. What happens? From the day of Pentecost onward Peter is a transformed man. Very suddenly, at the point of his greatest weakness, he has grown. Now what he says is wise and weighty, and he is the anchor man, as we would say, of the early church, the real rock man. (The Greek form of his name, *Petros,* means "rock.") Now he is fulfilling the role to which the name Jesus gave him had pointed. He still made mistakes. Paul calls attention to one of them in Galatians 2. But in the shaping of his character there had been a sudden and dramatic advance.

Now think about John. When Jesus first knew John, John was a fierce fellow. Jesus nicknamed him Boanerges, "son of thunder" (see Mk 3:17). I guess John was one of those men with great, black, bushy eyebrows that meet in the middle. He had zeal, but it was a savage, fierce zeal. At the end of John's life, however, we find him writing three letters into a situation in which some folks were claiming to be more spiritual than others, including himself, and had split churches over it. John writes to folk who had remained loyal to the apostolic teaching in order to reassure and encourage them. In this situation, where we might have expected John to knit his brows and speak fiercely about those who had left, we find in him instead the gentleness and restraint that mark him out as the apostle of love. He still sees spiritual issues in black and white, and censures the separatists as absolutely wrong. There is still a zeal for the Lord in everything he says. But the gentleness of love marks his spirit.

What has happened? Over the years, gradually, one would suppose, John has been so transformed that no longer is he a son of thunder but he breathes instead the pure spirit of Christlike affection and concern. This is growth in grace, but it is a different process from the sudden transformation seen in Peter.

Those who compare themselves with each other, says Paul in one place, are not wise. One reason why this is so is that God does not deal with us all on just the same points, at just the same time, nor at just the same pace. If we want to measure ourselves, let us rather ask, What am I able to do because I am a Christian living in the faith and strength of Christ today that I was not able to do before I was a Christian? It is no great thing if a person who was nice before being converted remains nice afterward. But it is a triumph of grace when a person like Peter, who was unstable as water before Pentecost, is turned into a strong, steady man, or when a man like John, whose ferocity required rebuke at least once (see Lk 9:54-56), becomes a paragon of love.

Mistake number three is *to suppose that growth in grace is automatic,* something you need not bother about because it will look after itself or something that is guaranteed if you are a professional minister, missionary or church officer. The enemy wants to encourage all who seek to serve God to take it for granted that as we do our job we will automatically grow and mature in Christ and therefore need not bother about sanctification at all. He wants to encourage us to think this way because if we are not striving to grow, we are actually in danger of doing the opposite, namely, shrinking behind the role we play.

Growth in grace means, among other things, that you are becoming more richly and robustly *human* than you were before. That is part of what it means to be changed from one degree of glory to another, so that more and more you will bear the image of Jesus Christ, the perfect person. Humanness is hard to pin down, but it certainly has to do with empathy, sympathy and alertness in our relationships; warmth, creativity and integrity in our attitudes; and wit, humor and gaiety in our spirits; as well as with the J-O-Y formula of the Sunday school (Jesus first, others second, yourself last). Christlikeness includes all these qualities, and all need to be deliberately sought or they will not be found. And it is only as they are found and ripen in us that we truly grow in grace. Again I say: growth, though often unconscious, is not automatic and is not likely to occur where it is not thought about and prayed for.

We clergy, I think (I speak as one), have often erred greatly here. We have not aimed at personal growth in grace, and we have missed it. We have instead concentrated on our role, and as individuals we have so often shrunk as we have played it, so as to become midget human beings behind a fraud façade, like the Wizard of Oz. My wife has sometimes had to say to me, "I don't want your ministry; I want you." What she is telling me when she says that is that I have been treating her impersonally and officially rather than leveling with her and letting her level with me as spouses should. She is right to insist on that, both for her sake and for mine, for impersonal attitudes to one's nearest and dearest argue spiritual shrinkage rather than growth.

Here is an Anglican limerick:

To his bishop a rector once said,
"May I take off my collar in bed?"
His bishop said, "No,
You may not do so;
You must wear it until you are dead."

The serious point reflected here is that many clergy do in fact seem to play their role twenty-four hours a day and to neglect the quest for personal maturing in Christ. To myself and to others (not just Anglicans, either) I say this as a warning: growth in grace has to do with our personal life as distinct from the role we play in church or elsewhere. We must not assume that growth will look after itself, and act as if it need not be our conscious concern.

Qualities of True Growth

Now a specific word about some of the dimensions of growth, those Christlike qualities that will increasingly appear in us if we are growing in grace.

1. One grows in the spirit of praising. Those who are growing in grace give themselves more and more to praise and worship, and grow less and less self-absorbed and self-concerned. There is a kind of balancing effect that operates here, like the up-and-down of the scale pans on old-fashioned weighing machines, or like a child's seesaw. If your pride and self-centeredness are increasing, your concern for praising God will be diminishing. But if your passion for praise is growing, then your sense of your own importance will be declining. You will then be following in the footsteps of Paul, who, writing to the Corinthians about A.D. 57 or 58, spoke of himself as the "least of the apostles," who, writing to the Ephesians about A.D. 61 or 62, spoke of himself as "less than the least of all saints" and who, writing to Timothy about A.D. 65 or 66, spoke of himself as the "chief of sinners." These phrases show how his estimate of himself was going down. Meantime, in his letters he constantly breaks out into doxology, which shows how passionately his heart sought to exalt and praise God. The lesson we learn from Paul here is that there is no growth in grace without increase in the spirit of humble praise.

2. *One grows in the spirit of enduring.* Or as the English Bible has for centuries rendered it, one grows in patience—steady endurance when the pressure is on. You see this in the Savior as his enemies closed in on him and the opposition increased toward the end of his ministry. That did not stop him. He endured. You see the same endurance in the apostles and in the heroes of church history and in everyone today who is growing in grace. Hebrews was a letter written to Christians under pressure, Jewish Christians who had to run the gauntlet of persecution from unconverted Jews. The writer says to them, "You need to persevere so that when you have done the will of God, you will receive what he has promised" (Heb 10:36), and that is a word for us all. What we learn from Hebrews here is that there is no growth in grace without increase in power to endure.

3. *One grows in the spirit of loving.* It is in the spirit of loving that we care for others and actually lay out our time, trouble, strength, prayers and every other resource to help them. The Lord Jesus is our model here. This was the kind of ministry he had throughout. He always lived in terms of the principle that it must be God first, others second, oneself last. Even on the cross, in his final agony, he was still

concerned for others. When they nailed him to the cross, he prayed for the soldiers who were doing it. As he hung on the cross, he saw his mother and told John to look after her. When the penitent thief spoke to him, he listened, cared, discerned the man's real faith and encouraged him with the promise "Today you will be with me in paradise" (Lk 23:43). This was love giving itself to the uttermost. The truth that we learn from Jesus here is that there is no growth in grace without an increase in selfless love.

4. *One grows in the spirit of contending*—that is, standing for God's truth against error. The one who grows in grace becomes increasingly ready to fight for God's truth in order to benefit God's people, with a combination of firmness and love, as Paul did when he wrote to the Galatians and the Colossians. His was a fighting spirit, but not the spirit of the firebrand who fights irresponsibly and cantankerously and disrupts churches, nor the spirit of the cross-grained Christian you can never get along with. It was, rather, the spirit of pastoral contention, battling for truth in theological warfare for the sake of people and their spiritual welfare. The insight we gain from this aspect of Paul's ministry is that there is no growth in grace without an increase in the tenacity that defends and commends the truths by which the church lives.

The Way of Growth

Finally, what are the means of growth whereby this maturing work of God is carried on in your life and mine? Theological textbooks normally speak of "the means of grace," a medieval phrase that the Reformers held on to in order to express the thought that here are particular activities through which God works to transform and ripen our lives.

The means of grace are commonly listed as follows. First comes *the Bible,* preached and received, heard, read, studied, meditated on, taken to heart, applied to oneself, stored up in memory, used as a guide for life. Second comes *prayer,* the regular exercise of communion and fellowship with God in praise, petition, intercession, thanksgiving, complaint, conversation, contemplation and whatever other modes of prayer God may lead us into. Third comes *worship* with the Lord's people, particularly at the Lord's Supper but also in hearing the Word regularly proclaimed and joining in the prayers and the vocal praise. Fourth comes *informal fellowship* and interchange as one member of the Lord's family ministers to another. Fifth comes *discipline,* not primarily in the unhappy but sometimes unavoidable form of judicial process and excommunication, but primarily in the form of discipling and nurture, with pastoral and spiritual direction, and the practice of what are nowadays called the disciplines of the spiritual life. (For one of the best treatments of these, see Donald S. Whitney, *Spiritual Disciplines for the Christian Life:* NavPress, 1991.)

As we approach these growth activities, we need to remember that growth comes from God through these means only as in using them we look beyond them to the Lord himself, asking him to bless them for our spiritual welfare. If we suppose that sharing in these activities has a magic of its own, we will be right off the track and will not grow in grace, however much we listen to sermons, pray and go through the motions of fellowship with God and fellow Christians. We must use the means of grace spiritually, as opposed to using them superstitiously. We are to grow precisely in the knowledge of our Lord and Savior Jesus Christ, to whom our eyes and our trust must always be directed. This is what it really means to grow in grace: that you have your eyes on the Lord and your hope in the Lord all the time, and so are coming constantly to "see him more clearly, love him more dearly, follow him more nearly," as the famous old prayer puts it.

Also we must remember that growth in grace is always growth by grace and under grace, never beyond grace, and grace means God enriching sinners. Sinners—that is who we are. We do not grow beyond grace. We never get to a point where we can cease to thank God for Calvary on a day-to-day basis or cease to humble ourselves before him as hell-deserving sinners. There is no sinless perfection in this life. Sinless perfection is part of the hope of glory. Here, the best the Lord enables us to do is always less than perfect, and we must constantly ask God to forgive what is defective in it. Can you accept that insight? It is basic, I believe, to a true view of this matter. If you have understood the second half of Romans 7, where we see Paul at his best, reaching out after perfection and then lamenting that his reach exceeds his grasp, you will appreciate what I am saying. However much we use the means of grace, we will never cease in this life to be sinners who must live daily by being pardoned and who could not live before God any other way. God forbid that we should ever be found thinking of ourselves in any other terms!

Real growth in grace through the Spirit will bring us consciously closer to Jesus Christ day by day, and that indeed will be one of the signs that God really is at work in our lives. As we "see him more clearly, love him more dearly, and follow him more nearly," we will grow in the knowledge of Jesus our Savior, sin-bearer, example, master and friend, who is himself the source of all the strength and power we need to follow in his steps. Such growth will honor God and be a supreme blessing to our souls. May it be yours and also mine.

7

SOME LESSONS
IN PRAYER

I REMEMBER BEING JOLTED BY THE REQUEST THAT I WRITE SOME-
thing on "my path of prayer." This was not because the topic was
off the beaten track. I had often quoted Robert Murray
M'Cheyne: "What a man is alone on his knees before God, that he is,
and no more." With M'Cheyne I believe that prayer is the spiritual
measure of men and women in a way that nothing else is, so that how
we pray is as important a question as we can ever face. Nor did the
jolt come from not having anything to say about prayer. It is a topic I
have written on with some frequency and one that no teacher of my
type ever leaves alone for long.

What was it then that jolted me? The little word *my*. The requested
topic was *my* path of prayer. Was I being asked to describe how I pray on
the assumption that I am good at it and might well be taken as a role
model? That would never do. I would not want anyone to settle for praying
as feebly, fitfully and ineptly as I feel I do. My heart said that trying to
describe what I do in prayer would be like telling the world how I make
love to my wife. Parading such intimacies would be nasty exhibitionism

on my part and would pander to the unspiritual, voyeuristic interest in others' spiritual experience that is unhappily widespread today. To join the psalmist in telling what the Lord had done for my soul (Ps 66:16) would be one thing, but to spotlight my own performance in prayer would be something else—a sort of spiritual striptease, entertaining perhaps but certainly not edifying. So I decided to do what I am going to do now, namely, write about the path I seek to follow when I pray, never mind how well or badly I actually perform at those times.

I start with the truism that each Christian's prayer life, like every good marriage, has in it common factors about which one can generalize and also a uniqueness that no other Christian's prayer life will match. You are you, and I am I, and we must each find our own way with God. There are no instructions for prayer that can work for us like a do-it-yourself manual or a cookbook, where the claim is that if you follow the directions, you can't go wrong.

Praying is not like carpentry or cooking. It is the active exercise of a personal relationship, a kind of friendship, with the living God and his Son, Jesus Christ, and the way it goes is more under God's control than under ours. Books on praying, like marriage manuals, are not to be treated with slavish superstition, as if perfection of technique is the answer to all difficulties. Their purpose, rather, is to suggest things to try. And as in other close relationships, so in prayer: you have to find out by trial and error what is right for you, and you learn to pray by praying. Some of us talk more, others less; some are constantly vocal, others cultivate silence before God as their way of adoration; some slip into glossolalia, others make a point of not doing so; yet we may all be praying as God means us to do. The only rules are to stay within biblical guidelines and, as Dom John Chapman put it, "pray as you can and don't try to pray as you can't."

Prayer Principles
Biblical guidelines for prayer are of two sorts: principles and models.

Here I would like to look at some theological principles.

First, Christian prayer is *communion with God through conversation.* It is an exercise of faith responding through grace to what one knows of the Father, the Son and the Spirit. It is prompted and fueled mainly by three things: (1) gratitude and adoration, which evoke thanks and praise, (2) awareness of need, both one's own and others', which calls forth confession, petition and intercession, and (3) the desire, present in every regenerate heart, that God should be honored and glorified, which leads to the kind of prayer that Scripture calls extolling or exalting him. The goal of Christian prayer is not to manipulate God into doing our will but to further the doing of his will, in our own lives as much as anywhere else. Petition, based on promise, is the essence of such prayer, which God delights to inspire, to hear and to answer.

While from one standpoint praying is the most natural thing a Christian ever does, since crying to the heavenly Father is a Spirit-wrought instinct in him or her, prayer is always a battle against distractions, discouragements and deadenings from Satan and from our own sinfulness. Prayer is not easy, and although spontaneity is of its essence, we have to make a dogged discipline of it, or else it will get crowded out—Satan will see to that! Should it degenerate into a formal routine, lacking inward concentration upon God and positive desire for his gifts and his glory, it would not be real prayer at all. Only through the energizing Holy Spirit, who gives the awareness and desire from which prayer springs, the thoughts and words in which it is voiced and the persistence in it that God commands, does prayer ever become all that it is meant to be. That is why Scripture summons Christians specifically to pray "in the Holy Spirit" (Eph 6:18; Jude 20).

I said this principle of prayer as conversation was familiar. Yet I wonder if I was right. Outside the evangelical tradition, contemplative rather than petitionary notions of prayer seem to prevail, and within evangelicalism a quietist stream of thought about communion with God flows steadily. Many conceive of prayer in terms of Whittier's hymn:

> Drop thy still dews of quietness
> Till all our strivings cease;
> Take from our souls the strain and stress
> And let our ordered lives confess
> The beauty of thy peace.

Praying then becomes in essence a quest for tranquillity. Others rejoice to read and recommend *Prayer* by the Lutheran pietist O. Hallesby, a book of which Donald Bloesch has justly written:

> Despite Hallesby's awareness of struggle in the life of prayer, the quietist, mystical element is more dominant than the evangelical one in his spirituality. Too often it seems that for him the struggle is not an anguished cry but a painless surrender. The work of the Spirit is so emphasized that human endeavour seems small in comparison. Prayer for Hallesby is more a friendly colloquy than an unceasing battle. Although he speaks of wrestling in prayer, he makes clear that we wrestle not with God but with ourselves, with the distractions of the world. The essence of prayer for Hallesby is "an attitude of our hearts towards God," a "holy passivity." (*The Struggle of Prayer,* 1980, p. 151)

I find the idea very common today that God calls us to abandon not simply self-justifying, self-assertive endeavors but all exerting of effort as such, that responsive relaxation is always the way to real intimacy with God and experience of his power. And that, I confess, bothers me.

In the mid-1940s, as a new Christian I tried to embrace this popular quietism and found it simply unreal. I nearly went out of my mind wondering what was wrong with me. Then I met the writings of the Anglican J. C. Ryle, the Puritan John Owen and the Reformer John

Calvin, which showed me that biblical Christian experience, whatever else it is, is active battling throughout—inwardly against the flesh (Gal 5:16, 24), outwardly against the world (Rom 12:1-2; 1 Jn 2:15-17), and both inwardly and outwardly against the devil (1 Pet 5:8).

Awareness and acceptance of the fight, these authors said, is itself a gauge of spiritual authenticity and vitality, and no Christian gets out of the second half of Romans 7 till he or she leaves this world. They also showed me at the practical level a truth that P. T. Forsyth later theologized for me in his great little book *The Soul of Prayer:* God may actually resist us when we pray in order that we in turn may overcome his resistance and so be led into deeper dependence on him and greater enrichment from him at the end of the day (think of the wrestling Jacob and the clamoring Job and of the parable of the unjust judge).

So now I reject the teaching that promotes passivity—intellectual, emotional or volitional—as based on a misunderstanding of Bible teaching about faith and as being both unspiritual and unhealthy. I see true prayer, like all true obedience, as a constant struggle in which you make headway by effort against various kinds of opposition. And however much you progress, you are always aware of imperfection, of incompleteness and of how much further there is to go. I have maintained this for half a century, but I fear it remains a minority view.

Biblical Models of Prayer

The Bible records hundreds of models of prayer—150 psalms, the Lord's Prayer and the prayers of saints from Abraham to Paul.

When we examine these models, we might well think of Thomas Fuller, who said that the prayers in the Anglican liturgy are like big clothes that parents buy for their children to grow into. The same can be said with yet more truth of the transcripts of holy hearts in action that these biblical prayers present. The Lord's Prayer in particular shows the pattern of goals and desires to which all truly Christian praying conforms. In my own praying, I find it salutary to ask myself again and again, Have my prayers spelled out what is in the Lord's Prayer? Has "hallowed be thy name—thy kingdom come—thy will be done" been the thrust of the things I have said to God? Also, I have found that to go through the Lord's Prayer, amplifying and specifying each clause (what the Puritans described as "branching" and C. S. Lewis called "festooning") is an infallible way to restart prayer when I get stuck or when I am struck dumb by the feeling that all I say to God is empty and meaningless.

As for the psalms I am always intrigued to find how Christians relate to them, for it took me years after my conversion to feel at home in them. Why? For two reasons, I think. First, the view of life as a battle, of which I wrote previously and which the psalms embody, took longer to root itself in my heart than in my head. And beyond that, the middle-class misconception that tidiness, self-conscious balance and restraint are essentials of godliness—a misconception that makes most of the psalms seem uncouth possessed both my head and my heart for even longer. More and more, however, the psalmists' calls for help, their complaints, confessions of sin, depression, celebrations of God, cries of love for him, challenges and commitments to him and hopes placed exclusively in him (all eggs in the one basket) have become the emotional world of my prayers. I now think this is how it should be for everyone.

The model of prayer that I seek to follow can be described in this way. First, it is a *conversation.* I am privileged to talk to God as a man to his maker, a servant to his master, a son to his father, a friend to his friend (see Jn 15:13-16; 20:17).

Second, it is a *trinitarian* exercise. I pray to the Father through the mediation of the Son and the enabling of the Holy Spirit. I may speak also to the Son and the Spirit directly when this is appropriate, namely, when I am praying about something that Scripture specifies as the direct concern of either.

Third, prayer is a *response,* the human side of a two-way fellowship. The triune God whom Christians love and serve communicates, as it were, by letter (the Bible), and we reply, so to speak, by phone (prayer). One day we will see our Lord and speak face to face, but for the present our relationship goes on as described.

Fourth, prayer is a *doxology,* that is, a matter of giving God glory and worship. The desire to honor and exalt God and see others doing the same ("Hallowed be thy name") is at the heart of prayer.

Fifth, prayer takes the form of a *two-tone address,* in which praise prompted by a vision of God (who he is, what he has done, what he will do) alternates with petition evoked by a sense of need.

Sixth, prayer is an *exertion.* The Holy Spirit's help, without which we could not pray at all, does not make lifting our hearts to God and concentrating on him any less hard. Praying aloud helps, and history records that Puritans, Methodists and leaders like Charles Finney prayed when they could at the top of their voice. (It is, after all, only natural to raise your voice when you are pleading with someone, human or divine.) One Puritan clergyman had a farm with a prayer room, where he prayed so loud that everyone on the farm could hear everything he said to God about them. We are told that this did them much good, but it is an example I would hesitate to follow. Let private prayer be private (see Mt 6:5)! Yet praying aloud certainly helps concentration, even if you only mutter.

Seventh, prayer is a means to *energy.* Spiritual alertness, vigor and confidence are the regular spinoff from earnest prayer on any subject. The Puritans spoke of prayer as oiling the wheels of the soul.

Finally, prayer is a *reward,* for recognizable answers to prayer bring joy and encouragement as nothing else does.

The Practicalities of Prayer

There are several things that help us in very practical ways to pray. To start with, we can count on *the Holy Spirit's help.* We should seek from

God the requests to make in each situation and recognize that it is the Holy Spirit's task, in addition to the rest of his ministry in our prayers, to guide us as we lay facts before the Lord. Often we enjoy no special leading and are only enabled to pray for needs in general terms, but sometimes the Spirit prompts very specific requests and leads us to make them with unusual confidence.

Here, for what they are worth, are two personal instances. Once the theological college of which I was principal was to be closed by episcopal order. The community fixed a day of prayer about it. Two hours into the day I found I knew exactly what to ask God for: a merger with another college on specific terms so unusual as to seem unrealizable. I could share this with no one at the time, but I held to the vision as best I could, and within a year all I had been led to pray for had happened. Glory to God! In another instance a friend was in the hospital for exploratory surgery. Cancer symptoms were present. Many prayed. Laying the situation before God, I found myself drawn (for the only time in my life, so far) to pray specifically and confidently for a miracle of healing. Walking home from church on Sunday morning and praying thus, I felt I was being told that the prayer was heard and I need not continue to press it. On Monday the operation revealed no trace of cancer. Once more, glory to God! We must always be consciously open to be led by God in the things we pray for.

We can also benefit from *the link between meditation and prayer.* Meditation, which as I use the word means thinking about God in God's presence, is a helpful preparation for speaking to God directly, and one that we seem regularly to need. In this world interviews with famous people are handled with some ceremony, both out of respect for the persons themselves and also in order to gain the most benefit from the interview. To rush to God randomly babbling about what is on our mind at the moment, with no pause to contemplate his greatness and grace and our own sinfulness and smallness, is at once to dishonor him and to make shallow our own fellowship with him. I, for one, want to do better than that.

Like others, I find it also good to preface my prayers about needs by reading Scripture, thinking through what my reading shows me of God, and turning that vision into praise before I go further. A little reverent thought about God before opening our mouths to address him makes a lot of difference in the quality of fellowship with him that follows. Remembering and reviewing the character of God is never wasted time. It is, rather, a vital means of *knowing* God, just as prayer itself is.

We need not be discouraged by *the problem of supposedly unanswered prayer.* I say "supposedly" because I challenge the supposition. While God has not bound himself to hear unbelievers' prayers, his promises to answer the prayers of his own children are categorical and inclusive. It must then be wrong to think that a flat no is ever the whole of his response to reverent petitions from Christians who seek his glory and others' welfare. The truth must be this: God always acts positively when a believer lays a situation of need before him, but he does not always act in the way or at the speed asked for. In meeting the need, he does what he knows to be best when he knows it is best to do it.

The parable of the unjust judge shows that God's word to his elect concerning the vindication for which they plead is "wait" (Lk 18:1-8), and he may say "wait" to other petitions as well. Christ's word to Paul, "My grace is sufficient for you, for my power is made perfect in weakness," when Paul had sought healing for his thorn in the flesh (2 Cor 12:7-9), meant no, but not simply no. Though it was not what Paul had expected, it was a promise of something better than the healing he had sought. We too may ask God to change situations and find that what he does instead is to give us strength to bear them unchanged. But this is not a simple no; it is a very positive answer to our prayer.

I remember a scene from my childhood. As my eleventh birthday approached I let my parents know by broad hints that I wanted a full-size bicycle. They thought it was too soon for that and therefore gave me a typewriter, which was in fact the best present and became the most treasured possession of my boyhood. Was not that good parenthood and a very positive answer to my request for a bicycle? God too allows himself to improve on our requests when what we ask for is not the best.

Wrote John Newton:

I asked the Lord that I might grow
In faith, and love, and every grace;
Might more of his salvation know,
And seek more earnestly his face.

I thought that in some favored hour
At once he'd answer my request;
And, by his love's constraining power,
Subdue my sins, and give me rest.

Instead of this, he made me feel
The hidden evils of my heart,
And let the angry powers of hell
Assault my soul in every part.

"Lord, why is this?" I trembling cried,
"Wilt thou pursue thy worm to death?"
" 'Tis in this way," the Lord replied,
"I answer prayer for grace and faith."

"These inward trials I employ
From self and pride to set thee free,
And break thy schemes of earthly joy,
That thou may'st seek thy all in me!"

Do we always recognize the answers to our prayers?

Finally, we should not forget *the preciousness of partnership in prayer.* I have in view here not the wider fellowship of prayer meetings, scriptural and excellent as that is, but the special benefit of praying with a like-minded Christian who is committed both to God and to you. The Puritans would speak of the need and value of a "bosom friend," a person with whom you can and do share everything, and who can pray with you and for you in a way that ministers to you. In these days of relational awareness, their point surely needs no argument. Everyone who has ever prayed with a "bosom friend" knows that it is true. Happy then is the one who finds such a partner, and stupid is the person who never seeks one. In prayer, as in many other activities, it is good when we can travel two by two.

8

COME &
WORSHIP

W

E ARE CONSTANTLY TOLD THAT WORSHIP IS THE SU-
preme Christian activity. True, no doubt. But what is
worship? Our culture knows nothing about worship and
dismisses it as something Christians do in church in which it is not
interested, so if we ourselves, as children of our culture, are clueless
about worship at this present moment, it should come as no surprise.
Recognizing this possibility, however, I will take nothing for granted
and begin at the very beginning. The first step toward forming sound
ideals of worship is to get clear as to its essential nature. So let us try
first to see what it is.

The history of the word gives us our answer. The noun *worship* is
a contraction of *worthship*. Used as a verb, it means "to ascribe worth"
or "to acknowledge value." To worship God is to recognize his
worthiness—to look Godward and acknowledge in all appropriate
ways the value of what we see. The Bible calls this activity giving
glory to God. It views this as our ultimate end and, from one point of
view, our whole duty. "Ascribe to the LORD the glory due his name"

(Ps 29:2; 96:8). "Whatever you do, do it all for the glory of God" (1 Cor 10:31).

Scripture views the glorifying of God as a sixfold activity: (1) praising God for all that he is and all his achievements, (2) thanking him for his gifts and goodness to us, (3) asking him to meet our own and others' needs, (4) offering him our gifts, our service and ourselves, (5) learning of him from his Word, read and preached, and obeying his voice, and (6) telling others God's "worth" by public confession and testimony to what has been done for us. We might say that these basic elements of worship can be phrased as follows: (1) "Lord, you are wonderful," (2) "Thank you, Lord," (3) "Please, Lord," (4) "Take this, Lord," (5) "Yes, Lord," and (6) "Listen, everybody!" The psalms abundantly illustrate all six.

Praise to God and Praise of God

Worship, then, taking it in its broadest sense, includes more than is sometimes realized: petition as well as praise, preaching as well as prayer, hearing as well as speaking, actions as well as words, obeying as well as offering, loving others as well as loving God. However, the primary acts of worship are those that focus on God directly—those in which God is to us not simply "he" but "thou." This means that we must not imagine that work for God in the world is a substitute for direct fellowship with him in praise and prayer and devotion. We often stress that bearing witness of Christ to others, from one point of view, is an act of worship glorifying to God, and evangelism is indeed a matter of high importance. We need to realize, however, that other acts of worship in which we talk not merely *about* God but *to* him matter even more. To deal with our neighbor in love is a basic duty. Equally, however, we cannot overstress that to hold fellowship with God in love is a duty even more basic.

Great as the second great commandment is, the first is greater. Acts of communion with God in which his worth is acknowledged, so to speak, to his face, are the true heartbeat of living faith. Moreover, it is by these acts of direct communion that Christians gain vision and vigor for their mission in the world. "He prayeth best who loveth best" is true, but "he loveth best who prayeth best" is a deeper truth still.

Before me as I write are a set of suggestions from a student author for delighting your loved one on Valentine's Day. One suggestion is "Write a letter . . . about when you first met, what your reactions were, what you've been through since, and how you feel about him or her today." Another is "Write a poem, . . . if you don't think you're up to that, . . . use a poem that someone else has written." Christianity is a kind of love affair with our loving Lord and Savior, and the more days we turn into spiritual Valentine's Days by talking to the Lord about our relationship with him along the lines suggested by the letter, drawing help from the Psalter, the hymnbook and the poems of people like George Herbert, the richer and more joyful the relationship itself will become. By expressing love, worship renews love, and the renewing of love to our Lord and to the Father is the greatest joy any Christian ever knows.

The New Testament sees the Christian church as a people saved to serve, and it regards prayer and praise, with "the grace of our Lord Jesus Christ" as its central theme, as the basic form of Christian service. Believers, says Peter, have become by grace "a holy priesthood, offering spiritual sacrifices acceptable to God through Jesus Christ, . . . that you may declare the praises of him who called you out of darkness into his wonderful light" (1 Pet 2:5, 9). There may be a reference in this last phrase to proclamation before others, in evangelism, but the main thing in view seems certainly to be the pouring out of praise before God, in glad remembrance of his greatness and goodness and grateful recitation of his marvelous doings. Similarly, the writer to the Hebrews urges, "Through Jesus . . . let us continually offer to God a sacrifice of praise—the fruit of lips that confess his name" (13:15).

Praise is the church's prime task, for the goal of all God's redeeming work, so Paul tells us, is "the praise of his glorious grace" and "the praise of his glory" (Eph 1:6, 14). In Revelation 4, twenty-four elders (probably representing the whole church of Old and New Testament times, the company headed by the twelve patriarchs and twelve apostles) worship God, saying, "You are worthy, our Lord and God, to receive glory and honor and power, for you created all things" (4:11). And in the next chapter they sing, "Worthy is the Lamb, who was slain" (5:12). Here is the substance of Christian worship, in both this world and the next. It is the declaring of the worth of God and of the Lamb, the glory of creation and the greater glory of the cross.

Worship is the church's central task. It is therefore every Christian's lifework, in the sense of his or her prime vocation. It is not drudgery. On the contrary, as we have already seen, it is the source of the believer's highest delight. That is not an overstrained platitude but sober truth. Unconverted people find the outward motions of worship tedious and boring, but to the regenerate, worship is a joy. It will be so in heaven when we see our Lord; it can be so already on earth. We in the Anglican tradition remind ourselves of this each Sunday as we say or sing to each other: "Let us heartily rejoice in the strength of our salvation." Such joy is not only for Anglicans; all Christians should be sharing it. If we know God as our Savior, then all the exercises of worship will generate joy, as many of the Psalms show with great vividness. For worship is natural—we might even say instinctive—to those who are born again. It is the most satisfying thing one ever does. Never are Christians so fully themselves or so happy as when their hearts are drawn out in the worship of God.

The relation of child to father or wife to husband is meant to be a love relationship in which the voicing of love by the beloved marks the perfecting of the relationship itself and brings the supreme joy of it to both sides. God's children, whom the New Testament often pictures as married to Christ, are similarly caught up in a love relationship and find their highest joy in talking to God of his love to them and theirs to him. This was the point of the Valentine's Day analogy that I urged earlier, and it is a fact—a hard fact, a solid fact, a universal fact—of Christian experience. If it is not a fact of our own experience, we need to ask ourselves whether we are Christians at all. Certainly if we are unacquainted with the joy of praising God for our salvation, we are not qualified to discuss standards and styles for anyone's worship, today, tomorrow or whenever. Much current debating on worship styles—whether prayer in church should be liturgical or extempore, cool and laconic or passionate and rhetorical, whether to address God as "thee" or "you," whether to sing old didactic hymns or modern praise songs, and so on—remains disappointingly shallow, just because the sheer joy of using words to express love and appreciation for God is left out of the discussion.

The Spirit of Worship

It is already clear that worship is essentially *response*—response to God as he reveals himself to us. Worship thus presupposes knowledge. Christian worship takes place only where there is knowledge of the biblical truths of creation and redemption and of the Jesus of the New Testament made real to us by the Holy Spirit. "Yet a time is coming and has now come," Jesus told the Samaritan woman, "when the true worshipers will worship the Father in *spirit and truth*" (Jn 4:23). By this he meant that through his personal ministry as sin-bearing Savior, master and friend, worship was being put on a new basis and lifted to a new level. To worship God in spirit is to worship him from the heart, "in the Spirit" (Rev 1:10), by an outgoing of mind and will and affection toward him. To worship God in truth is to approach him on the basis of his self-disclosure in the One who elsewhere said, "I am the way and the truth and the life. No one comes to the Father except through me" (Jn 14:6).

When we worship in spirit and in truth, we rise above, first,

Spiritless worship, consisting only of externalities of ritual and cere-mony, and second, Christless devotion, marked by ignorance, unreal-ity and superstition, based on the asserting of falsehood or the denying of fact. True worshipers will praise and pray freely, spontaneously and from their hearts, but at the same time their worship will be rigorously controlled by the realities of revelation.

Those that worship in spirit and in truth, Christ goes on to tell the Samaritan woman, "are the kind of worshipers the Father seeks" (Jn 4:23). God desires worship that is a true response to the truth made known in Jesus. From this it follows that what finally matters about the church's forms for worship is not whether they are new or old, liturgical or extemporaneous, but whether they embody revelation in such a way as to further worship that meets this requirement.

The way a church worships is, in fact, supremely important not only because deficient worship displeases God (though this is reason enough, in all conscience) but also because of its reflex action on the church itself, for good or ill. Worship that embodies a full measure of evangelical truth will edify those who join in it. It will also act as a stabilizer in times of doctrinal decline.

In the first part of this century the liberal landslide in theology made deeper and more damaging inroads among the "free" churches than it did in liturgical churches like the Church of England. Why the differ-ence? Partly because the truths of which liberalism lost hold—sin, incarnation, atonement, regeneration, verbal revelation, supernatural grace—were so fully expressed in the Book of Common Prayer, which thus acted as a brake on doctrinal drift. A sound prayer book is a boon when the pulpit goes astray! On the other hand, heterodox forms of worship naturally instill mistaken ideas into the minds of those who use them. The Catholic Mass, for instance, did this for many centuries. Liturgical patterns mold worshipers' minds at a deep, presuppositional level. Their didactic potency is thus greater than it is possible to calculate.

Many worship patterns are found in Christian churches, and most of them are right and good. Thus it is our wisdom to learn versatility, so that we can enter into them all. The minimum specifications are that there should be praise and thanksgiving to God, confession of sin and proclamation of pardon for the penitent, reading and exposition of the Word of God, petition for daily needs, and regular administration of the Lord's Supper. The acid test is whether one's involvement, whatever the procedural form, is wholehearted. Without wholeheartedness, liturgical refinement means nothing, and when worshipers are wholehearted, crudeness of style will not detract from the glory of God.

So come and worship! Reality, as distinct from formality, in worship brings vitality to Christians and churches as nothing else does. Worship is in any case rehearsal for heaven, and what can be more important than that? An epitaph for a Puritan contained the line "Heaven was in him, before he was in heaven." If we give ourselves to worship, there will be grounds for saying that of us too.

9

FELLOWSHIP
IN THE
CHURCH

THE BODY IS A UNIT, THOUGH IT IS MADE UP OF MANY PARTS; and though all its parts are many, they form one body. So it is with Christ. . . . Now you are the body of Christ, and each one of you is a part of it" (1 Cor 12:12, 27).

These words are part of an illustration of which Paul was fond. Indeed, it was his standard illustration for making clear the nature of the inner life of the church. There is one church universal that is invisible in its own nature. It is the company of those who have living faith in Christ and so are united to each other because they are united to him. But that church becomes visible wherever the people of God, either many or few, meet together to do the things the church does: worship, pray, maintain the ministry of the Word, spread the gospel, fellowship, celebrate the sacraments and share the things of God. So Paul, writing to the local church at Corinth, says, "You are the body of Christ." *You!*

He would in fact say the same thing to every congregation he was privileged to address. Each local congregation is a microcosm of the church universal. Therefore, when people look at this or that congregation, they should see the life of the world church concentrated in that one place.

What sort of life should it be? Body life, the life in which all the limbs (the Greek word for *parts* or *members* literally means "limbs") are contributing to the welfare of the whole. Our bodies give us trouble when any part is not working properly. When the parts work together, however, the body is a wonderful thing. In the same way, Paul wants us to understand that the life of a church is a wonderful thing as in the power of God's Spirit each limb, joint and muscle does its best and contributes to the health of the whole. As he says in Ephesians 4:16, "The whole body, joined and held together by every supporting ligament, grows and builds itself up in love, as each part does its work."

Today the phrase *church growth* commonly refers to an increase in membership or attendance. But the New Testament perspective is that God is interested in quality even more than he is interested in quantity. He calls for the evangelizing of the world, but most of all he is concerned that the functioning of the church, the company of the faithful, should always and everywhere bring glory to him as this supernatural life of fellowship with Christ is displayed, lived out, deepened and ripened.

A Lively Church

First Corinthians 12—14 is a passage of Scripture that makes painful reading for thoughtful believers. Why? Is it because Corinthian public worship as described in chapter 14 was such a chaotic uproar? Is it because of the apparent unseemliness of services in which many folk were talking at once, some in ecstatic gibberish, and in which some women were screeching to be heard above the general noise? Because, in other words, it was a scene of great confusion? That is how it seems to have been, as some of Paul's statements in chapter 14 show. But it is not for this reason that I speak of these chapters as painful. They make painful reading because, whatever evils they confront us with, they do at least show us a local church in which the Holy Spirit was working in power. So reading the passage makes one painfully aware of the impoverishment, inertia and deadness of so many churches at the present time.

If our only reaction to these chapters is to preen ourselves and feel glad because our churches are free from Corinthian disorders, we are fools indeed and ought to think again. I fear that many of our churches today are orderly simply because they are asleep. And in many cases I fear it is the sleep of death. It is no great thing, is it, to have perfect order in a cemetery?

The Corinthian disorders were due to an uncontrolled overflow of the Holy Spirit. There was real carnality and immaturity in these people. It was deplorable, and Paul censures it strongly. But this must not blind us to the fact that they were nevertheless enjoying the ministry of the Holy Spirit in a way in which most of us today are not. Remember how, at the start of the letter, Paul wrote, "I always thank God for you because of his grace given you in Christ Jesus. For in him you have been enriched in every way—in all your speaking and in all your knowledge. . . . You do not lack any spiritual gift" (1 Cor 1:4-5, 7).

This was not just empty politeness! Paul meant what he said. He always did, and this statement is no exception. The Corinthians really had been enriched by Jesus in the manner described. So when they met for fellowship, they brought with them gifts and contributions in abundance. Whereas congregations today too often gather in a spirit of unexpectant apathy, scarcely aware that they come to church to receive, let alone to give, these Corinthians met with eagerness, excitement and expectation, anxious to share with their fellow believers the "manifestation of the Spirit" that was theirs (12:7). Paul says,

"When you come together, everyone has a hymn, or a word of instruction, a revelation, a tongue or an interpretation" (14:26).

Public worship at Corinth was thus the opposite of a drab routine. Every service was an event, for every worshiper came ready and anxious to share something God had given. Paul gave regulations not for creating this state of affairs but for handling it in a way that was orderly and edifying once it had arisen. The state of affairs was itself the spontaneous creation of the Holy Spirit in that church. And when the Corinthians met for worship, the presence and power of God in their midst was an experienced reality.

This is the basic dimension of spiritual revival. Within the Corinthian fellowship there was a sense of the presence of God that struck awe into people's hearts, just as had happened at Jerusalem in the early days. The knowledge of God and the sense of God's presence among the believers was too strong for casual, irresponsible contact. That is how it always is in revival times, and that is how it was at Corinth. The awareness of God that was there at the church's meetings gave every word that was spoken in God's name heart-searching power.

On this Paul utters what is perhaps the most remarkable throwaway line in the whole New Testament. "If an unbeliever or someone who does not understand comes in while everybody is prophesying [I think this means 'preaching the gospel'], he will be convinced by all that he is a sinner . . . and the secrets of his heart will be laid bare. So he will fall down and worship God, exclaiming, 'God is really among you!' " (1 Cor 14:24-25). Paul affirms this as a certainty! His confidence is breathtaking.

Could that seriously be said to any church today? Say it in most of our churches, and the only reaction will be "How marvelous if that would happen! It is not happening here." Yet in revival times this has happened over and over again. It obviously had happened at Corinth more than once that a casual visitor, coming by accident into a church service and hearing what was said in God's name, had his or her heart searched and broken and was transformed and went out a renewed man or woman. Paul could not have expected the Corinthians to believe his throwaway line had it not been so.

The Corinthian disorderliness was grievous, that we grant. But the Corinthian church was being carried along by a great surge of divine life. Disorder, as such, is demonic. It is not in the least to be desired. But it remains a question whether Holy Spirit life, with all its exuberance and risk of disorder, is not preferable to spiritual deadness, neat and tidy though that deadness might be.

Three centuries ago, in his discourse on spiritual gifts John Owen reviewed the Puritan revival of the early seventeenth century and frankly acknowledged the misuse of spiritual endowments that had disfigured the era.

> By some, I confess, they [gifts] have been abused; some have presumed on them; some have been puffed up with them; some have used them disorderly in the churches, and to their hurt; some have boasted. . . . All which miscarriages also befell the primitive churches. [But] I had rather have the order, rule, spirit and practice of those churches which were planted by the apostles, with all their troubles and disadvantages, than the carnal peace of others in their open degeneracy from all these things.

I must agree. Give me life with all its disorder rather than death with its tidy inertia.

Our Common Life

So if the Corinthian church, with all its excesses, is nevertheless a true example of spiritual liveliness, where is our example of fellowship? Let us explore what the New Testament says about fellowship, or sharing, which is what fellowship really is. What does the thought of fellowship suggest to you? A cup of coffee in the church hall? Gossip on the steps outside after the service? Conversation at a Christian family camp? Touring Scotland or the Holy Land with a bus full of church people? We often say we have had fellowship when all we mean is that we have taken part in some Christian social enterprise. Yet the fact that we share social activities with other Christians does not of itself imply that we are having fellowship with them. That may not be so at all.

I am not denying that there is a place in the life of God's people for activities of this kind. My only point is that to equate these activities with fellowship is an abuse of Christian language, and a dangerous one. It fools us into thinking that we are thriving on fellowship when all the time our souls may be starving for lack of it. It is not a good sign when a person sees no difference between sucking sweets and eating a square meal. Equally, it is not a good sign when Christians see no difference between social activities in Christian company and what the New Testament calls fellowship in Christ.

Fellowship is one of the great words of the New Testament. It denotes something that is vital for our spiritual health and central to the church's true life. We notice, as we read the New Testament, that fellowship features in the first description of the young church: "They devoted themselves to the apostles' teaching and to the fellowship" (Acts 2:42).

What is meant here? Gossip? Cups of tea? Tours? No. What is being referred to is something of quite a different order and on quite a different level. The New English Bible has an illuminating paraphrase of these verses: "They met constantly to hear the apostles teach, and *to share the common life* [that is the paraphrase for fellowship], to break bread, and to pray. A sense of awe was everywhere.... All whose faith had drawn them together held everything in common. ... With one mind they kept up their daily attendance at the temple, and, breaking bread in private houses, shared their meals with unaffected joy, as they praised God" (vv. 42-47). That is fellowship as the New Testament understands it, and there is clearly a world of difference between that and mere social activities.

I believe that one of the reasons why great sections of the modern church are so often sluggish and feeble, compared with our counterparts of one or two centuries ago, is that the secret of fellowship has been lost. Christ rebuked the Laodiceans for complacently supposing that they had all they needed when they were actually in a state of spiritual bankruptcy. I believe he would rebuke us for talking so glibly about the happy fellowship we have with each other when lack of fellowship really is one of our glaring shortcomings. A body in which the blood does not circulate properly is always unhealthy, and fellowship corresponds to the circulation of the blood in the body of Christ. We gain strength through fellowship and lose strength without it. We grow in fellowship. We regress if we live in isolation from one another. How then should we analyze fellowship and focus it before our minds?

The Greek word for *fellowship* comes from a root word meaning "common" or "shared." So fellowship means common participation in something either by giving what you have to the other person or receiving what he or she has. Give-and-take is the essence of fellowship, and give-and-take must be the way of fellowship in the common life of the body of Christ.

The Dimensions of Fellowship

Christian fellowship is *two-dimensional,* and it is first vertical before it can be horizontal. We must know the reality of fellowship with the Father and with his Son, Jesus Christ, before we can know the reality of fellowship with each other in our common relationship to God. In his first epistle, John writes, "Our fellowship is with the Father and with his Son, Jesus Christ" (1:3). But he also says, "We proclaim to you what we have seen and heard, so that you also may have fellowship with us" (1:3)—fellowship with us in our fellowship with God. Fellowship with the Father and the Son is the experience of one who is truly a limb in the body of Christ. The person who is not in fellowship with the Father and the Son is no Christian at all, and so cannot share with Christians the realities of their fellowship. This vertical dimension is presupposed when we think of the horizontal dimension of fellowship.

The fellowship of sharing with one another what we have received from the Lord is a spiritual necessity. God has not made us self-sufficient. We are not equipped to keep going on our own. This is often illustrated from a coal fire. Put the coals together and the fire burns; separate them and each goes out quickly. So it is in the body of Christ. We are made not for isolated and self-sufficient living but for togetherness in dependence on each other.

The writer to the Hebrews, seeking to stir up the flagging faith and zeal of those harassed Jewish Christians, urges them (among other things) to have more fellowship: "Let us not give up meeting together, as some are in the habit of doing, but let us encourage one another— and all the more as you see the Day approaching" (Heb 10:25). The church will always flourish where there is strong fellowship. The church will always be stagnant, moribund and ineffective where there is no fellowship. There may be orthodoxy, but this is more than orthodoxy. It is the shared life that the people of God are called to live.

Christian fellowship is also the family activity of God's people. In a good family there is plenty of sharing among the siblings. In the family of God also that is the way it is meant to be. Like fellowship with the Father and the Son, it is two-way traffic, give-and-take. When it is fellowship with the Father and the Son, we receive the gift of a relationship with God and we give ourselves to the Father and the Son in grateful response. In the horizontal dimension of fellowship, sharing with our fellow Christians, we give as God has given to us, and we receive.

So Christian fellowship is seeking to share with others what God has made known to us, while letting others share with us what they know of him. This acts as a means of finding strength, refreshment and instruction for one's own soul. Gratefully one receives what others share. Equally, one labors to give. And in the giving, no less than in the taking, one finds renewal and strength.

We see this in Paul. A very remarkable Scripture, I think, is Romans 1:11-12. Paul declares to the Romans, people that he has never met before: "I long to see you so that I may impart to you some spiritual gift to make you strong." Then lest he give the impression that he thinks the fellowship between him and them is one-way only, all give and no take, he hastens to add as a kind of explanation of what he has just said, "that is, that you and I may be mutually encouraged by each other's faith."

Preachers know this experience. Special joy comes from opening the Word of God to people who are obviously hungry for it and obviously appreciative of it. The knowledge that people have received what the preacher has sought to give does his heart good. Those who preach must then, however, be open to receive whatever ministry comes back to them from those to whom they have spoken. Proud aloofness here would be deadly.

In Romans 1 Paul is envisioning not only the joy of knowing that the Romans will receive the things he is sharing; he also wants to know the joy of receiving from them what the Lord has given them. God forbid that we should be so self-sufficient in our pride and vanity that we should be unwilling to receive and ready only to give. When that happens, fellowship becomes a sort of ego trip. This attitude of "I'm the one who gives, but I don't need to take" has ruined the ministry of more pastors than I can number. Paul was not too proud to look forward to receiving and so being strengthened in fellowship with the people to whom he ministered. So I say to those in the ministry, as I say to everyone who rejoices to share the things of God: seek from the Lord the humility that is willing to take and to be ministered to, as well as to minister.

A Threefold Definition
Christian fellowship, then, is an expression of both love and humility.

It springs from a desire to bring benefit to others coupled with a sense of personal weakness and need. It has a double motive: the wish to help and the wish to be helped, the wish to edify and the wish to be edified. It is thus a corporate seeking by Christian people to know God better through sharing with each other what individually they have learned already. We seek to do others good, and we seek that others will do us good.

We can therefore say three things about fellowship. First, it is *a means of grace.* Through fellowship and in fellowship one's own soul is refreshed and fed by the effort to communicate one's knowledge of divine things, to come and pray for others, and to receive from God through them.

Second, fellowship is *a test of life.* Fellowship means opening one's heart to one's fellow Christians. The person who is free to eschew pretense and concealment when talking to other believers is the one who is being open and honest in dealings with God. He or she is the one who is walking in the light, as John puts it in his first letter ("If we walk in the light, as he is in the light, we have fellowship with one another," 1 Jn 1:7). If we are not walking in the light, we do not have fellowship with one another. If we are not letting the light of God shine full on our lives, we will never have free fellowship with others because we will be unwilling to open up to them. After all, why would we be willing to tell them the shameful secrets of our hearts when we are not prepared to open up to God and let him deal with these things? Those who will not walk in the light with God will never walk in light with other believers.

Third, fellowship is *a gift of God.* The NIV translates Paul's blessing in 2 Corinthians 13:14 like this: "May the grace of the Lord Jesus Christ, and the love of God, and the fellowship of the Holy Spirit be with you all." The kind of fellowship of which I am speaking comes only as God's gift in and through the Holy Spirit. It has as its motive to love our brothers and sisters in Christ as an expression of our love to the Lord, and it involves real openness with each other and real reliance on each other. It is only where the Holy Spirit has been given, where we are spiritually alive to God and anxious to grow in grace ourselves and help others do the same that such fellowship will be a possibility. It is only as the Spirit enables us that we will actually be able to practice it.

When does fellowship become a reality? Whenever two or more Christians desiring to help each other to know God better share with each other such knowledge of God and experience of God as they individually possess. It happens when they take responsibility for each other in that sharing situation, when they advise, pray for, encourage and seek in every way to uphold their brother or sister in his or her life and testimony.

This can happen in many circumstances. It can happen in preaching. It can happen as we pray together. It can happen in group Bible study. It can happen in talk between friends over a meal. It can happen in talk between husband and wife at home. But what happens in every case will be the same thing: the Lord's presence and power will be realized, and we will prove afresh through the words, attitudes, actions and love of another Christian the truth of that promise from the Lord Jesus Christ to be present where "two or three come together in my name" (Mt 18:20). That promise applies no less to informal acts of fellowship than to public worship. It finds fulfillment when Christians meet together to share casually just as it does at the stated hours of worship on Sunday.

The Lessons of History

Some would ask whether this teaching about fellowship is new or whether it has been taught throughout the history of the church. To that I have these responses.

First, even if this understanding of fellowship was not an emphasis at all times in the past, it should be an emphasis in our churches today.

What we are talking about is the form and fruit of spontaneous Holy Spirit life, wherever it exists. In fact, wherever new life from God has come to the churches, this sort of fellowship has begun to appear spontaneously, without anyone's needing to search the theological journals, famous writings or whatever to find precedents for practicing it.

But of course, this understanding of fellowship *was* a reality in the history of the church. For example, the Puritans often met to talk about divine things and to pray. Sharing and praying together at home was for them a basic activity of Christian family life. And they urged from time to time that every believer should seek from God the priceless gift of one "bosom friend," the friend who can listen to our deepest thoughts, support and pray for us, and hold us accountable. Over and above ordinary pastoral care from the clergy, so they insisted, this kind of close peer relationship is something every Christian needs.

Fellowship also played a key role in the Wesleyan revivals. Wesley was converted in a fellowship meeting, a Moravian Pietist Society meeting in Aldersgate Street, London. Wesley, Whitefield and other leaders of the eighteenth-century evangelical awakening founded fellowship groups—"societies," as they were called then—in order to "maintain the glow" God had brought into the hearts of their converts. They insisted that one could not keep Christians on an even keel, alive and bubbling over with the life of God on a day-to-day basis, unless they belonged to such societies.

Again in revivals that began in East Africa in the 1930s, immediately there were revival fellowships. They just happened. The folk who had come alive to God met together spontaneously to share, pray, sing and encourage each other in the Lord. They did it because they found themselves wanting to do it. They do it still, and the revival still goes on.

It seems that every time there has been spiritual quickening the pattern of Malachi 3:16 has been fulfilled: "Those who feared [knew and loved] the LORD talked with each other." They got together for this purpose. I think that the small-group movement of our time, if rightly guided by true ideals of church life, holds tremendous potential for renewal. The fellowship pattern is there, ready-made. What it needs is the touch of God. The full potential of these small-group structures is yet to be realized.

Second, Christian leaders have known this principle of fellowship and have urged the importance of groups. Take George Whitefield. He was a great evangelist and in himself a unifying figure of the English-speaking evangelical movement in the eighteenth century. He led for thirty-five years. He preached eighteen thousand sermons at least, averaging ten a week, and gave many more informal discourses. By common consent his ministry had more impact on the eighteenth-century scene than that of anyone else. Wesley and Jonathan Edwards were the first to admit it. Whitefield wrote:

> If we look into church history we shall find that as the power of God prevails Christian societies and fellowship meetings prevail proportionately. My brethren, let us plainly and freely tell one another what God has done for our souls. To this end you would do well, as others have done, to form yourselves into little companies of four or five each and meet once a week to tell each other what is in your hearts, that you may then also pray for and comfort each other as need shall require. None but those who have experienced it can tell you the unspeakable advantage of such a union and communion of souls. And none that I think truly loves his own soul, and his brethren as himself, will be shy of opening his heart in order to have the advice, reproof, admonition and prayers of his brethren. A sincere person will esteem that one of the greatest blessings.

Whitefield considered it part of the preacher's goal to foster the fellowship of believers in groups.

Third, in fellowship of this sort, biblical theology can restrain excesses that, in fact, have often crept into some of these groups. I spoke of accountability, but I would now add that it must be an accountability under God. We must never forget that God alone is Lord of the conscience. One error that has been widespread in certain circles is the insistence that every Christian must be in a relation of absolute obedience to some other Christian. Here the idea of accountability has been taken too far. It has become a domination of the authority figure over the one under authority. This is real tyranny, for the authority figure now stands as lord of the conscience in God's place, just as medieval priests used to do. God alone is Lord of the conscience, and fellowship relations of the kind of which I am speaking must be practiced under the ultimate and acknowledged authority of the Lord, who from his Word shows his children what is right and what is wrong for their lives. In fellowship, as in all else, the appeal to Scripture is necessary and decisive.

Spiritual Gifts in the Fellowship of Believers

Fellowship is carried on through the reality of spiritual gifts. In these days much has been taught about spiritual gifts. I will limit myself to brief remarks on the theology and practice of spiritual gifts.

What is a spiritual gift? It is in essence a God-given capacity to express or minister Christ so that those to whom service is rendered will see Christ and grow in Christ to his glory. It may be a gift of speech, behavior, conduct or service in any form. It may be a practical gift of relieving needs, Samaritan-style, just as it may be the teacher's gift of explaining things from the Word. But whatever it is, it is a God-given ability to make Christ known. When gifts are exercised in the power of the Spirit by whom they are bestowed, the reality of the situation is this: Christ himself, on his throne but through his Spirit in us, is ministering still to people as he did in the days of his flesh. We become his mouth, his hands, his feet to fulfill each day his ministry to others by exercising the spiritual gifts we have been given.

Usually others see our gifts better than we see them ourselves.

Usually others can tell us better than we are able to discern by introspection what we can and cannot do for the Lord. Realizing then that the finding and use of gifts is fellowship business, we should ask others to watch us and tell us what our gifts are, and so be guided by them.

Our charismatic friends may be wrong in their idea that the sign gifts that authenticated the apostles are maintained by God in every age, including this one. (I deal with charismatic experience in the next chapter.) But my charismatic brothers and sisters, it seems to me, are absolutely right to stress the importance of every member ministering in the body of Christ. So I ask you, what is your ministry? What is your gift or gifts? What are the things you can do to express and communicate Christ? If you have never sought the answer to that question, begin to seek that answer now in the fellowship of the Christians who know you best, and go on from there.

A healthy view of spiritual gifts will avoid the last hindrance to body life that I wish to discuss. That hindrance I call clericalism, which is the state of affairs in which the minister says, "You leave the spiritual ministry to me; that's my job," and the congregation says, "Yes, that's absolutely right. So we will." Clericalism can also be expressed the other way. The congregation may say to the minister, "We hired you to do the spiritual ministry. Get on with it! That's the job you're paid to do." And the minister then says what a minister should never consent to say, namely, "I accept that, and so I will." Either way, clericalism is in effect a Spirit-quenching conspiracy. For those who serve God as clergy and pastors, it is necessary to insist on the principle of every-member ministry.

We should seek the state of affairs reflected by a church letterhead pattern that (thank God!) has become quite common during the last few years. The letterhead states: (1) the name of the church, (2) "ministers: the congregation," and (3) "assistant to the ministers," or some such phrase: the name of the pastor! That is how it should be in every local assembly.

In a church some years back I saw on the door of the pastor's study a little plaque saying: Head Coach. That was right also!

Now for your own sake, for the sake of your church, for the glory of our Lord Jesus Christ, for the blessing of the world through churches that are really alive, I beg you to seek fellowship in its fullness. Do not rest until every-member ministry is a reality in your own church or fellowship. Love one another; pray for one another; end those wretched divisions and the cliquishness and other things that quench the Spirit and prevent fellowship from being what it ought to be. Seek true fellowship, and do not rest until it becomes a reality for you through the power of the Spirit of God. Then our churches will really be alive, beacons for Christ in the place where God has set them, and they will grow in the full scriptural sense of that word.

10

RENEWAL & CHARISMA IN THE CHURCH

WHENEVER ONE RAISES THE ISSUE OF FELLOWSHIP AND church growth, the question whether one is for or against the charismatic movement comes up. It is a polarizing, party-minded, Corinthian sort of question. I usually get around it by saying I am for the Holy Spirit. But why is it asked so often and so anxiously? Perhaps it is because some evangelicals feel threatened by charismatics, having been crowded by them and having perceived (they would say) weaknesses and errors in what they do. I wish to review and assess these, and then zero in on a number of significant insights noncharismatics can profitably gain from charismatics.

First, a word of general orientation. The charismatic movement has its Roman Catholic, Eastern Orthodox and Protestant components, and it focuses on celebrating the ministry of the Holy Spirit. The evangelical movement, by comparison, plays a role in most older

Protestant bodies and focuses on a longing to see God's revealed truth about Jesus Christ reform and renew Christendom. These two movements, charismatic and evangelical, are overlapping circles. Many evangelicals define themselves as charismatics; many charismatics define themselves as evangelicals; their concerns converge.

Charismatic theology may look loose and naive beside evangelical formulations, sharp-honed as these are in consequence of nearly five centuries of controversy. But the two constituencies are plainly at one on such evangelical distinctives as personal conversion to Christ, lives changed by the Spirit's power, learning about God through Scripture, boldly expectant prayer, small-group ministry and a love for swinging singing.

Most of what is distinctive in charismatic theology comes from the older Pentecostal movement, which sprang up at the start of this century out of the yet older Wesleyan tradition. Though charismatic Christianity tends to treat experience rather than truth as primary and embraces people with many nonevangelical beliefs, it remains evangelicalism's half sister. This may explain why evangelical reactions to charismatic renewal seem sometimes to smack of sibling rivalry.

Commonly Voiced Concerns

Why do some evangelicals feel worried by the charismatic movement? When that question is asked, mention is regularly made of the following.

1. Irrationality in glossolalia. Charismatics see their "tongues" as God-given prayer languages, perhaps angelic. But to those who would address God only intelligibly and who know from professional linguistic scholars (who are unanimous on this) that glossolalia has no language-character at all, it can seem shockingly silly, self-deceived and irreverent. Granted, earlier diagnoses of glossolalia as a neurotic, psychotic, hypnotic or schizophrenic symptom are not tenable. On the contrary, the evidence reveals glossolalia as in most cases psychologically and spiritually health-giving, so far as one can judge. Yet many still find the thought of making nonsense noises deeply disturbing and are unnerved by people who are exuberantly sure that this is what God wants them to do.

2. *Elitism in attitudes.* Charismatics see their kind of communal spirituality as God's current renewal formula and themselves as his trailblazers in this. Hence they naturally talk big about the significance of their movement and may leave impressions of naive and aggressive arrogance, as if they thought only charismatics mattered in the sight of God.

3. *Judgmentalism in theology.* Protestant charismatics (Catholics less so) tend to theologize their experience in terms of recovering primitive standards of Christian spirituality through seeking and finding what was always available but what earlier generations lacked faith to claim, namely, Spirit baptism and sign gifts (tongues, interpretation, miracles, healing and, as charismatics believe, prophecy also). This restorationism, the equivalent in spirituality to Anabaptist ecclesiology, implies that noncharismatics are substandard Christians and that the only reason why they lack charismatic experience is that through either ignorance or unwillingness they have not sought it. Such beliefs, however gently and charitably stated, are inescapably threatening.

4. *Disruptiveness in ministry.* The charismatic movement often invades churches in the form of a reaction (sometimes justified) against formalism, intellectualism and institutionalism, in favor of a free-wheeling experientialism. Such a swing of the pendulum is bound both to win converts and produce division. Frustration-fed reactions always do. Many churches have split because charismatics have either walked off or, in effect, have driven others out, in both cases with an apparently good conscience. Other churches contain charismatic cliques who keep a low profile but may scheme to move things their way. Pastors in particular naturally feel threatened.

Evaluating These Concerns

Judgmentalism evokes judgmentalism. Many Christians have written off the charismatic movement entirely as a delusive and perhaps demonic distraction. But inasmuch as it produces conversions, teaches people to love Christ, the Bible and their neighbors, and frees them up for worship and witness, demonic delusion cannot be the true story. A more discerning estimate is required.

Charismatic "restorationism" (belief that God is currently restoring all first-century experiences) certainly seems doubtful. There is no way to establish the disciples' Spirit baptism at Pentecost as a normative experience for all later believers. Indeed, quite apart from the fact that as an experience we know very little about it, its uniqueness rules that out. Nine o'clock on Pentecost morning was the singular, unrepeatable moment when the promised Spirit first began his new-covenant ministry of communicating communion with the glorified Christ. Since that moment all Christians have enjoyed this ministry from conversion on (Acts 2:38-39; Rom 8:9-11; 1 Cor 12:12-13). Because the disciples became believers before Pentecost, their experience had to be "two stage" in a way no later Christian's can ever be.

Moreover, though the subsequent experience of those who testify to having received Spirit baptism may be far richer than it was before the event, it does not seem significantly to differ from that of devoted people who have not known this "second blessing."

Nor is there any way to make good the claim that the sign gifts that authenticated the apostles (Rom 15:18-19; 2 Cor 12:12; Heb 2:3-4) are now restored. The nature of those gifts is in many respects uncertain and must remain so. We cannot be sure that current charismatic phenomena fully correspond to them. For instance, charismatics commend private glossolalic prayer, but New Testament tongues are signs for use in public; charismatics who claim healing gifts have a spottier success record than did Christ and the apostles, and so on.

Yet one can doubt restorationism (which in any case is not approved doctrine among Roman Catholic and German Protestant charismatics) and still rejoice in the real enrichment that charismatics have found in seeking the Lord. Their call to expectant faith in the God who still on occasion heals supernaturally and does wonders can be gratefully heard, and their challenge to seek radical personal renewal can be humbly received without accepting all their theology. We should be glad that our God does not hide his face from those who seek him, neither from charismatics nor noncharismatics, until their theology is correct. Where would any of us be if he did? And we should not refuse to learn lessons from charismatics while contesting some of their opinions.

I urge that a better way to theologize what is called or miscalled Spirit baptism is as follows. It is an intensifying of the Spirit's constant witness to our adoption and inheritance (Rom 8:15-17). It is a deepening of the communion with Father and Son of which Christ spoke (Jn 14:21-23). It is an increase in the knowledge of Christ's love that Paul prayed the Ephesians might enjoy (Eph 3:16-19). And it is a renewing of that unspeakable joy in Christ (1 Pet 1:8) of which the Puritan John Owen wrote, "There is no account to be given, but that the Spirit worketh it when and how he will; he secretly infuseth and distills it into the soul, filling it with gladness, exultations, and sometimes with unspeakable raptures of mind."

Vivid awareness of the divine love seems always to be the essence of the Spirit baptism experience, whatever its adjuncts, as it has been also of countless comparable experiences that have been differently labeled. These have included sealing with the Spirit among the Puritans; entire sanctification among the Wesleyans; the noncharismatic Spirit baptism affirmed by Finney, Moody and Torrey; the Keswick experience of consecration and filling with the Spirit; the mystics' "second conversion"; and other meetings with God to which no such brand name as Spirit baptism has been given. I propose the same theological account of God's work in all such experiences as being biblically viable and fitting the facts.

Charismatic Contributions

Despite some unhappy theology, the charismatic movement overall bears marks of genuine spiritual renewal, and though it or sections of it may have lessons to learn in doctrine, it has its own lessons to teach with regard to practice. Doubtless these lessons are not unique. But when God has brought new life to so many through charismatic channels, it would be perverse conceit on the part of noncharismatics to be unwilling to look and learn.

The charismatic movement, like the evangelical movement, is a fairly self-sufficient, transdenominational, international network, with its own established behavior patterns, literary resources and leadership. How far to identify with all this or with what one's local charismatic community is doing is something that each individual must decide for himself or herself. But it seems to me that all Christians can learn from charismatics about the true meaning of ideals to which lip service is too easily given.

The first ideal: total worship. The charismatic conviction is that worshiping God should be a personal realizing of fellowship with the Father and the Son through the Spirit, and therewith—indeed, thereby—a realizing of spiritual oneness with the rest of God's assembled family. Liturgical structures therefore are loose enough to allow for spontaneous contributions and ad libs. They are also relaxed, informal and slow-moving enough to let all bask in the feeling of togetherness with God and with each other. In pace, in cultivated warmth and in its way of highlighting points by repetition, charismatic worship is to historic liturgy as Wagner and Bruckner are to Mozart and Haydn: romantic, in the sense of directly expressing attitudes and feelings, rather than classical, in the sense of focusing on excellence of form. The aim is total involvement of each worshiper, leading to total openness to God at the deepest level of one's being. To achieve this, charismatics insist, time must be taken; their worship meetings thus may be two or three hours long.

What does this say about the brisk, stylized sixty-minute canter—clergy and choir pulling along a passive congregation—that is the worship diet of so many Christians on so many Lord's days? All would no doubt protest that total worship was their aim too, but are all as realistic and perceptive as charismatics in seeing what this involves?

The second ideal: total ministry. It was Paul and Peter who first affirmed that every Christian has a gift or gifts for use in the church (Rom 12:4-6; 1 Cor 12:4-7; Eph 4:7, 11, 16; 1 Pet 4:10). Thus the charismatics insist (making a point that is distinct from their claim that sign gifts are present) that every-member ministry, achieved by discerning and harnessing each Christian's ordinary gifts, should be standard practice in the body of Christ. Congregational behavior patterns must be flexible and decentralized enough to permit this.

There's the rub! Every-member ministry is an ecumenical shibboleth as well as a charismatic slogan these days, and few hesitate to mouth it. But are all as practical as charismatics in devising new structures and reshaping old ones so as to make it happen? No. In many churches the complaint is heard that the talents of gifted people lie unused, and obvious needs in personal and neighborhood ministry go unmet because the pastor insists on being a one-man band and will not treat his flock as a ministering team, in which some members do some things better than he. Charismatics as a body are past this blockage point in a way that radically challenges all who are not.

The third ideal: total communication. Charismatic worship is characterized by features that impress different people differently. These features include singing (both from books and "in the Spirit"), clapping, arm raising and hand stretching, the lead-passing ritual of glossolalia from one followed by interpretation from another, delivery of prophecies from God to the group, loose and improvisatory preaching, and corporate dialogue with the preacher by interjection and response. But while some will fault some of these items, none can fault the purpose they serve: to make all that God's people do together deepen their sense of God's presence and power and their openness to his leading at all points. When this is achieved in any measure, you have what Walter J. Hollenweger calls "atmospheric communication," an established revival phenomenon.

Without advocating the particular practices mentioned or any technique of "working up" meetings (for manufactured excitement never communicates God), I urge that the charismatic purpose is right. Charismatic practice, however haphazard it may seem on the surface, convicts the restrained, formal behavior in church that passes for reverence of not being the most vivid, lively and potent way of communicating the reality of God. Let all consider how "atmospheric communication" can best be effected.

The fourth ideal: total community. Community or fellowship, which means having Christ in common and sharing what we have from him, is a quality of Christian relationships that charismatics seek to maximize. Their distinction is that they share well, giving of both themselves and their substance generously, sometimes recklessly, to help others. In their prayer groups, their discipling relationships and their experiments in communal living, the strength of their desire to serve in love, whether wisely expressed or not, puts others to shame. And meanwhile, the vividness of their vision of the whole church as a great extended family, which is the body of Christ on earth, is magnificent.

Again the question that arises is not whether all should imitate the particular things charismatics do but whether their example does not expose halfheartedness in others who say they want community but settle for locked-up lives and never squander themselves in love. If it does, what steps will those others now take to put themselves right?

We have seen that some Protestants are hostile to the charismatic movement because they disagree with some strands of its teaching or because they feel it threatens them. Others, we know, patronize it as involving illusions that some people need that, therefore, should not be resisted, only ignored. These responses seem inadequate. The movement is forcing all Christendom to ask what it means to be a Christian and to be Spirit-filled. It is bringing into recognizably evangelical experience people whose ears were once closed to evangelical witness as such. As "egghead" radical theology invites the church into the wilderness of a new Unitarianism, is it not (dare I say) just like God to have raised up against it not a new Calvin or Owen but a scratch movement that proclaims the deity and potency of the Son and Spirit not by great theological acumen or accuracy but by the evidence of renewed lives and a changed lifestyle? A movement that by its very existence reminds both the world and the church that Christianity in essence is not words only but also a person and a power? Surely we see divine strategy here.

But whether or not I am right to think this is how Christians of tomorrow will see the charismatic renewal of today, I am sure we will all do well to try and learn the lessons spelled out here.

11

CHRISTIAN CITIZENSHIP

I
T IS COMMON IN SOME CHURCHES TODAY TO STATE THAT WHEN
we leave the service of worship, the worship that is service begins. It is a paradox of the Christian life that the more profoundly
one is concerned about heaven, the more deeply one will care about
God's will being done on earth. The Christians who show most passion
to serve others in this world are regularly those with the strongest hold
on otherworldly realities. This has always been true, whether we look
at ministers, missionaries, politicians, reformers, industrialists, phy-
sicians, people of wealth and power or ordinary layfolk.

Service to others, as an expression of love to them, is a Christian
priority. But citizenship is a form of service, as most Christians have
seen from the start. Despite the Marxist claim that religion anesthe-
tizes one to the needs of earth, we find that, other things being equal,
those whose citizenship is in heaven (I echo Paul's phrase in Philip-

pians 3:20) make the best citizens of any state, democratic or totalitarian, Christian or pagan, secular or even atheist.

The Biblical Basis for Public Activism

In the New Testament civic obligation is emphatically commanded alongside, indeed as part of, the obligation to serve God. When Jesus answered the question about taxpaying with the words "Give to Caesar what is Caesar's, and to God what is God's" (Mk 12:17), this was not a clever evasion of the issue but a clear acknowledgment that rendering what is due to the existing political regime is part of the Christian calling. When Peter in one breath says, "Fear God, honor the king" (1 Pet 2:17), he spotlights the same truth. Paul does this also when, in the course of his overview of the life of gratitude for grace that is true Christianity, he teaches the Roman Christians to "submit . . . to the governing authorities" (Rom 13:1) and tells them that "because of conscience" they should "give everyone what you owe him: If you owe taxes, pay taxes; if revenue, then revenue; if respect, then respect; if honor, then honor" (Rom 13:5-7).

Paul speaks of each state official as "God's servant to do you good" (Rom 13:4). Note that it is pagan Roman officials, from the emperor down, that he has in view! And he further explains that God instituted the state to maintain law, order, justice and "good." *Good* here evidently embraces protection and well-being and is thus not far removed from the opportunity to pursue happiness, which the American Constitution enshrines.

Hence, although Christians are not to think of themselves as ever at home in this world but rather as sojourning aliens, travelers passing through a foreign land to the place where their treasures are stored (see Mt 6:19-20; 1 Pet 2:11), Scripture forbids them to be indifferent to the benefits that flow from good government. Nor, therefore, should they hesitate to play their part in maximizing these benefits for others, as well as for themselves. The upholding of stable government by a law-abiding life and the helping of it to fulfill its role by personal participation where this is possible are as fitting for us today as they were for Joseph, Moses, David, Solomon, Nehemiah, Mordecai and Daniel (to look no further). We must see it as service to God and neighbor.

As one Christian member and former vice president of the European Parliament, Sir Frederick Catherwood, trenchantly put it: "To try to improve society is not worldliness but love. To wash your hands of society is not love but worldliness."

Some Misguided Christian Developments

Along with the laudable examples above, we must here note three developments in modern Christendom that have set up perplexing crosscurrents with regard to political duty. Each requires some discussion before we can go any further.

1. The politicized intentions of some Christian relativists. When I speak of Christian "relativists," I have in mind certain Protestants who treat biblical teaching not as God's revealed truth but as humanity's patchy pointer to God's self-disclosure, couched in culturally relative terms that today's Christians are not bound to use and voicing many sentiments that today's Christians are not bound to endorse.

When I speak of "politicized intentions," I mean that their goals reduce the Christian faith from a pilgrim path to heaven to a sociopolitical scheme for this present world. This scheme is often referred to as establishing God's kingdom on earth by ending society's collective sins of racism, economic and cultural exploitation, class division and denial of human rights. This agenda is intended to set up *shalom* (the Hebrew word for communal well-being under God).

What is wrong here? Not praying for *shalom* nor working for it as one has opportunity. Neighbor-love in the global village requires every Christian to do this and to do it on an international as well as a domestic scale.

But it is surely disastrous when Christian faith (our grasp of God's revealed purposes among men and women) and Christian obedience (our efforts to do God's revealed will) are reduced to and identified with human attempts at social improvement. The heart is cut out of the gospel when Christ is thought of as Redeemer and Lord, Liberator and Humanizer only in relation to particular deprivations and abuses in this world. This, however, has become the standard view of liberals and radicals among the Protestant leadership. It is expressed and reinforced by the World Council of Churches and the "liberation theology" of some Roman Catholics in Central and South America.

What has happened, putting the matter bluntly, is that clergy and laypeople in the mainline Protestant bodies have allowed themselves to reinterpret and redefine their basic religious values as political values. Thus they have secularized Christianity under the guise of applying it to life. In doing so, they have turned it more or less into a leftist ideology, in which even revolutionary violence and guerrilla warfare against lawful governments get baptized into Christ. A flow of semitechnical books expressing this viewpoint, the entrenching of it in liberal seminaries and the verbal dignifying of it as the discipline of "political theology" have made it respectable. Steady propaganda in its favor from Protestant denominational headquarters now leads many laity to equate the Christian citizen's role with pushing this program everywhere.

The basic mistake in all this is that Christianity's transcendent reference point has been lost. Those who revere Bible teaching as divine truth, who see Jesus in New Testament terms as first and foremost our Savior from sin, delivering us from wrath to come, renewing us in righteousness and opening heaven to us, and who view evangelism as the basic dimension of neighbor-love, ought to oppose social evils just as vigorously as anybody else. To do that is part of the practical Samaritanship to which all Christians are called, that is, the relieving of need and misery every way one can. But it is all to be done in the service of a Christ whose kingdom is not of this world and who requires humanity to understand this life, with its joys and riches on the one hand and its hardships and sorrows on the other, as a moral and spiritual training ground, a preparatory discipline for eternity. Lose that perspective, however, as the relativists of whom I am speaking have lost it, and the entire enterprise of neighbor-love goes astray.

2. *The pietistic inhibitions of some Christian absolutists. Absolutists,* as I here use the word, are those Protestants, Roman Catholics and Orthodox who believe that God's unchanging truth is given to the church in Scripture and that only by obeying this truth can one please God. They may be called Christian conservatives, or even conservationists, by reason of their unwillingness to recast or diminish the historic biblical faith. Among Protestant absolutists, many, perhaps most, would prefer to bc called evangelicals, since the gospel (the evangel) of Christ is central to their Christianity.

These people are *pietistic* in their concern about achieving holiness, avoiding sin, winning souls, practicing fellowship with Christians and opposing all the forces of anti-Christianity on the personal level. Pietistic inhibitions take the form of political passivity and unwillingness to be involved in any level of civil government. Some will vote but not run for office, others will not even vote, and all incline to treat political issues as not directly their business. Their stance as Christian citizens is thus one of withdrawal from rather than involvement in the political process.

Several factors seem to operate to bring this about. One is a reaction against the Social Gospel of the more liberal Protestantism such as was described above, from which evangelical pietists want to dissociate themselves as fully as possible. A second is a faulty inference from their eschatology (their view of the future), which sees the world as getting inevitably and inexorably worse as Christ's coming draws near and tells them that nothing can be done about it; therefore, it does not matter who is in power politically. A third factor, linked with this, is the stress laid on separation from "the world," with its moral defilements, its compromises of principle, and its earthbound, pleasure-seeking, self-serving way of life. Politics, thought of as a murky milieu where principles are constantly being sacrificed in order to catch votes and keep one's end up in the power game, is seen as an eminently "worldly" business and so off-limits for Christians. A fourth factor, potent though imponderable, is an individualism that resolves all social problems into personal problems and feels that civil government is unimportant since it cannot save souls. This makes these individuals fundamentally not interested in the political process at all.

But none of this will do. Whatever mistakes the Social Gospel may enshrine and however true it is that ministry in the church and evangelism should be our first concern, there remains a social and political task for Christians to tackle.

Even if the second coming is near, we can still, under God, make this world temporarily a little better if we try. In any case, the fear of not succeeding cannot excuse us from trying when God in effect tells us to make the attempt.

Further, while politics is certainly a power game, it has to be played if social structures are to be improved. Though it belongs to this world, it is still a sphere of service to God and people that is not intrinsically "worldly" in the proscribed sense. Moreover, political compromise, the basic maneuver, is quite a different thing from the sacrificing of principles, as we will see.

Finally, the individualism that destroys political concern is a kind of myopia blurring awareness of the benefit that good government brings and the damage that bad government does (think of Adolf Hitler, Pol Pot, the Gang of Four and the recent leadership in Serbia). No! Pietistic passivity cannot be justified, and its present practitioners need to be educated out of it. This negativism is no more valid a stance for the Christian citizen than was the politicized posture that we rejected earlier.

3. The political imperialism of some Christian biblicists. I have in mind here the crusading spirit that currently animates certain members of Bible-loving churches and fellowships. They might call themselves fundamentalist rather than evangelical, because they feel that the former word implies more of the uncompromising fighting stance.

Here there is no hesitation in announcing objectives and plunging into the hurly-burly of the political world in order to gain them. Problems arise, however, through the temptation to view the democratic power game as the modern equivalent of holy war in the Old Testament, in which God called upon his people to overthrow the heathen and take their kingdom by force. It is because of this temptation that I speak of political "imperialism."

In biblical holy war the heathen had no rights and received no tolerance, for God was using his people as his executioners, the human means of inflicting merited judgment. Viewed as a revelation of God's retributive justice (an aspect of his character that shines throughout the whole Bible), holy war made coherent, if awesome, moral sense. But holy war is no part of God's program for the Christian church. Leave retribution to God, says Paul in Romans 12:19. And holy war makes no moral or practical sense at all if taken as a model for Christian action in the political cockpit of a modern pluralistic democracy like the United States, Canada, India or Britain.

In a democracy you cannot govern except as public opinion backs you and retains you in office. Therefore the quest for consensus and the practice of persuasion with a view to achieving consensus are all-important. Riding roughshod over others as if they did not count will always have a self-defeating boomerang effect. Pressure groups that seek to grab and use power without winning public support for what they aim at will provoke equally high-handed opposition and will typically be short-lived.

Protestants may well rejoice that Roman Catholicism has now given up its long-standing conviction that error has no rights. Should

Protestants themselves now flirt with that discredited principle, however, there will soon be egg on their own faces. And the danger is constantly present. As the late Paul Henry pointed out in his *Politics for Evangelicals,* "righteous zeal" can be very "detrimental to the practice of politics. For 'true believers' of any stripe are always tempted to become hard-core ideologues seeking to impose their truths on society at large." Christian citizens, who ought to have strong beliefs about communal right and wrong, will always need to be careful here.

Why Support Democracy?

Representative democracy as we know it, in which the legislature, the judiciary and the executive have separate status, the public information services (media) are not under government control, the elected administration always faces an elected opposition, and popular elections on a one-person, one-vote basis recur at regular intervals, is not the only form of government under which Christian citizens have lived and served God. However, there is no doubt that from a Christian standpoint it is a fitter and wiser form than any other.

The Christian recommendation of democracy rests on two insights. The first is the awareness that government of the people, by the people, for the people, in an open community system that in principle allows anyone to qualify for any office, best expresses in political terms our God-given dignity and the worth of each individual.

The second is the perception that power must be limited. In this fallen world, as Lord Acton put it, all power corrupts and absolute power corrupts absolutely. Thus the separation of powers and the building of checks and balances into executive structures will limit the dangers of corruption, even if such procedures for restraint will never eliminate them entirely.

These Christian insights mesh with the worldly wisdom that sees that the more citizens can feel they have shared in making the decisions that now shape their lives, the more resolutely they will adhere to them. The pattern of government, therefore, that maximizes public consent will ordinarily be more stable than any other system.

Making Democracy Work

Christian citizens, then, may be expected to show a firm commitment to the principles of democracy and to see themselves as bound to do all they can to make democracy work. But that means conscientious commitment to the democratic process as the best way of decision making within the body politic.

In democracies that are philosophically and religiously pluralist, like those of the West, the democratic process that achieves consent out of conflict is vitally important. In this fallen world, conflict arising from limited vision and competing interests is an unavoidable part of the political scene. The intensity and integrity of the public struggle whereby a balance is struck between the contending parties then becomes an index of community health and morale.

The name given to the resolution of political conflict through debate is *compromise*. Whatever may be true in the field of ethics, compromise in politics means not the abandonment of principle but realistic readiness to settle for what one thinks to be less than ideal when it is all that one can get at the moment. The insight that compromise expresses is that half a loaf is better than no bread.

Give-and-take is the heart of political compromise, as compromise is the heart of politics in a democracy. To see this is a sign of political maturity. By contrast, a doctrinaire rigidity that takes up an adversarial position toward all who do not wholly endorse one's views and goals implies political immaturity.

Democratic decision making is as public a process as possible, and officials are expected to publish their reasons for action wherever this can be done without jeopardizing the future. But all major political decisions prove to be both complex in themselves and controversial in the community. This is inescapable for at least three reasons.

First, everyone's knowledge of the facts of every case is partial and selective. Second, values, priorities and opinions about the relative importance of long- and short-term results will vary. Think, for instance, of the debates that go on about conserving the environment. Third, calculations of consequences, particularly unintended and undesired consequences, will vary too, and many actions that seem right to some will seem wrong to others because they foresee different consequences. Because executive decisions regularly have unwelcome byproducts, they become choices between evils—attempts, that is, to choose the least evil and avoid evils that are greater. Think, for example, of the debate about using nuclear devices in war.

The Christian citizen must accept that in politics no black-and-white answers are available, but God wills simply that all be led by the highest ideals and ripest wisdom that they can discover. The case of Solomon (1 Kings 3) shows that God's gift to rulers takes the form of wisdom to cope creatively with what comes rather than ready-made solutions to all problems.

What Should the Christian Citizen Do?

The New Testament does not speak about active political participation for the very good reason that this was not an option for first-century believers. The Roman Empire was not a democracy, and many if not most Christians were not Roman citizens. They were a small minority from the lower end of the socioeconomic spectrum and were viewed as eccentric deviants from the older eccentricity of Judaism. They had no political influence nor any prospect of gaining any. (It took longer than the past two hundred years of American independence before the early Christians secured even political protection. Prior to Emperor Constantine, their faith was illegal and they lived everywhere under spasmodic persecution.) So the only politically significant things they could do were pay their taxes (Mt 17:24-27; 22:15-21; Rom 13:6-7), pray for their rulers (1 Tim 2:1-4) and keep the peace (Rom 12:18; 1 Thess 5:13-15).

Present-day representative democracy, however, opens the door to a wider range of political possibilities and thereby requires of us more in the way of responsible commitment than circumstances required in New Testament times. The required commitment may be summarized as follows:

1. All should keep informed; otherwise, we cannot judge well about issues, vote well for candidates or pray well for rulers. Political ignorance is never a Christian virtue.

2. All should pray for those in power, as 1 Timothy 2:1-4 directs. The secret efficacy of prayer, as Scripture reveals it, is enormous.

3. All should vote in elections and referendums, whenever expressions of public opinion are called for. We should be led in our voting by issues rather than personalities, and not by single issues viewed in isolation but by our vision of total community welfare. This is one way (real, if small), in which we may exert influence as the world's salt and light (Mt 5:13-16).

4. Some should seek political influence by debating, writing and working within the political party with which they are in nearest agreement. Clergy should not ordinarily do this, since it will be a barrier to the acceptance of their ministry by people who disagree with their politics. It is, however, very desirable that laypeople with political interest should see the gaining and exerting of political influence as a field of Christian service, alongside the fields of church life, worship and witness, with which they are likely at present to be more familiar.

5. Some should accept a political vocation. Who should do this? Those in whom interest, ability and opportunity coincide and on whom no rival career has a stronger claim. Also those with a vision for improving humanity's lot globally, advancing international peace, replacing unprincipled discrimination with justice and furthering pub-

lic decency should consider it. And finally, those who are prepared to work hard, with patience, humility, tolerance and integrity, fleeing fanaticism, riding out rebuffs and putting the public interest before their own should be encouraged. The Bible histories show that God wants some of his servants as professional politicians, leading and shaping society well, and the discovery that one is fitted for this role is a prima facie summons from God to go ahead and embrace it.

Let none, however, be starry-eyed at this point: the choice is costly. The political path is rough traveling. The goldfish bowl of public life exposes one constantly to pitiless criticism, and to live there requires resilience and involves major self-sacrifice. As Robert D. Linder and Richard V. Pierard have written in *Politics: A Case for Christian Action:*

> The work is often thankless and discouraging, and it sometimes means psychological strain and heartbreak for those involved in it. The problems are difficult, and, no matter what a politician does, invariably someone will be dissatisfied and complain about it. Every person in the community has the right to criticize the acts of any public official, and the critics have the advantage of hindsight, a privilege denied the decision-maker. . . . From a personal standpoint, political endeavor places heavy demands upon one's time, family and financial resources. Many friends will automatically assume that an individual is in politics for some ulterior motive, and they will reveal this by the knowing look or sly remark.

Politics is a power game, and the envy, hatred, malice and self-seeking duplicity that the power game regularly draws out of the sinful human heart is too familiar to need comment here. No politician of principle can expect an easy passage, certainly not the Christian.

But who ever thought that the fulfilling of any aspect of Christian vocation would be easy? The words with which Sir Frederick Catherwood ends his book *The Christian Citizen* are worth frequent pondering:

We must be humble and not opinionated. We must be prepared to find that we are sometimes quite wrong and be able to admit it. We serve our fellowmen because of our love for a Lord who gave his life for us, a debt which, however well we serve, we can never repay. So whatever we do, we do it from a sense of duty and because it is right. We do not, like the cults, claim instant satisfaction. We do not, like the salesmen, guarantee success. The Christian's timespan is not mortal. One sows and another reaps. One labors and another enters into his labors. One day with God is like a thousand years and a thousand years like one day. The Christian knows the meaning of patience and endurance. But he also knows the meaning of action.

This is the right formula for Christian politics, just because it is the right formula for every single part of the Christian life.

12

THE
UNTRUTH OF
UNIVERSALISM

THE GOSPEL IS "THE POWER OF GOD FOR THE SALVATION OF *everyone* who believes" (Rom 1:16). That is the universal claim of Christianity. God "commands *all* people everywhere to repent" (Acts 17:30). That is the universal summons of Christianity. Jesus said, "Go and make disciples of *all* nations" (Mt 28:19). That is the universal mission of Christianity.

The Influence of Universalism

The universalism of claim, call and commission is not in dispute. Very much in dispute, however, is whether the universal proclamation of redeeming grace for all who will receive it warrants or allows the hope that all who in this life, for whatever reason, have not accepted this message will ultimately find their place in the kingdom of grace. In ordinary use, the term *universalism* denotes the position of those who embrace this hope. It is in this sense that we will be using the word here.

Today universalism is a common belief throughout the world of liberal Protestantism. It was first broached as a serious theological point of view by the great scholar Origen in the early third century, and for two centuries made some headway, but it was condemned toward the end of the sixth century. It was then a discredited hypothesis that for centuries nobody took seriously. In mainstream Protestantism up to the nineteenth century, universalism was nothing more than an unorthodox minority view. But then things began to change.

The universalist dogma was maintained by the pioneer of liberalism, Friedrich Schleiermacher, and many followed in his steps. In an age of cultural optimism and boundless confidence in the future of humanity, the universalist spirit spread throughout the whole of Christendom. In our time, for the first time in Protestant history, missionary leaders as well as theologians in the major denominations are promoting the theory of universalism.

Universalists claim that they alone do justice to the reality of the love of God and the victory of the cross. Belief in any form of the doctrine of eternal loss or eternal punishment, they say, makes God a failure; indeed, some will go so far as to say that it makes him a devil. Is this so?

What are the implications of universalism? If all people will be saved, the urgency of evangelism is taken away. It then becomes possible to argue that other ways of loving your neighbor are more important than seeking first and foremost to win him or her to faith in the Lord Jesus Christ. So it becomes very easy to move away from the gospel of conversion to a merely social gospel.

Now consider the issue this raises. Throughout church history individual Christians have carried a burden of prayer for evangelism and missions and have pleaded with God night and day for those whom they saw as lost. They have prayed out of the vivid conviction that without conversion, all people are going to hell—irretrievably and irrevocably. In love and compassion they have gotten on their knees and asked God to have mercy and save souls. The question for us is, was this necessary? Was there any sense in it? Universalism has a bearing not only on what we say to people but also on how we pray for people. Prayer for God to save the lost is misguided if in truth no one is really lost at all.

Universalism has become a problem today because its personal appeal is so strong. Bible believers have traditionally viewed universalism as a teaching that is morally weakening and spiritually deadly. They have seen it as suggesting that one's conduct here does not matter and as encouraging false hopes of eternal life even though one does not repent and believe. They have historically recognized in universalism the modern form of Satan's lie in the garden, "You will not surely die" (Gen 3:4). Yet with world population growing by the billion and only a third of the human race making any kind of Christian profession, there can be few who do not sometimes find themselves wishing that universalism was true.

Universalism is a soothing doctrine. It is not pleasant to think that dear friends and relatives may be heading for eternal distress and torment. If we are normal Christians, we wish we did not have to live with this conviction. Universalism, on the other hand, is comfortable in a way that belief in eternal punishment can never be. And I am afraid that wishful thinking leads many of us to live and behave as if universalism were true, even though we would never subscribe to it in writing.

What the Bible Says

What has the Bible to say about the universalist hope?

Concerning the hope of the believer at death, there is no question on either side. How could there be when the New Testament is so exultantly clear about the glory of the believer's prospects? "There is now no condemnation for those who are in Christ Jesus" is the way Romans 8 opens; it closes by saying that nothing in heaven or earth can separate us from the "love of God that is in Christ Jesus our Lord"; and in the middle (v. 17) it tells us that we are "co-heirs with Christ" who will "share in his glory."

Our question, however, concerns the destiny of those who live "without hope and without God in the world" (Eph 2:12). What of them? The first eight chapters of the epistle to the Romans declare that they are under law, under sin, under wrath and under death. They are under law in the sense not merely that they are obliged to keep it but that they are destined to be judged by it. Sin, with its dynamic power of perversity propelling them out of the way of God into revolt and rebellion, shapes their lives. They are thus under God's wrath, that is, his holy hostility to sin and sinners that is being revealed from heaven against all human ungodliness and unrighteousness. Those who are under sin and under wrath are also under death. "The mind of sinful man is death" (Rom 8:6). "If you live according to the sinful nature, you will die" (Rom 8:13).

The mere juxtaposing of those two texts shows us that death in the Bible does not mean cessation of being. Rather, it means continued existence in a state in which one has lost something essential for the life that God made one to live. People are dead in one sense now, and they will be dead in a deeper sense hereafter. On this basis it is no surprise to find that the New Testament goes on to develop what seems to be a strong and incontrovertible doctrine of eternal punishment.

We are told in Jesus' parable of the sheep and the goats (Mt 25:46) that those whom the royal judge rejects go away into a final state of eternal punishment. This phrase is balanced in the last half of the verse by the reference to "eternal life," which is also a final state. Some would argue that the state of punishment is not unending. Yet the same Greek term is used in both cases. If "eternal life" refers to a state that is endless, then a parallel endlessness can hardly be excluded from what is meant by the corresponding and balancing phrase "eternal punishment."

The New Testament conceives of eternal punishment as consisting of an agonizing knowledge of one's own wrongdoing, of God's displeasure, of the good that one has lost and of the fixed state in which one now finds oneself. This doctrine of eternal punishment was taught in the synagogue long before our Lord took it up and enforced it in the Gospels. But the language that strikes terror into our hearts—weeping and gnashing of teeth, outer darkness, the worm, the fire, Gehenna, the great fixed gulf—this is all directly taken from our Lord's teaching. It is from Jesus Christ that we learn the doctrine of eternal punishment most clearly.

While the word *punishment* shows that it is the royal judge (Jesus himself) who decrees this destiny, we need to be clear that in every case it has been actually chosen by the one being punished. John says that some light from God reaches everybody, by general revelation if not through the gospel, and humankind is divided into those who approach the light, welcoming it, and those who hate it and shrink from it because they love darkness (see Jn 1:4-5, 9; 3:16-21). For pagans as for Christians, the day of judgment will mean deeper entry into the life they prefer—in their case, life without God, which has all along been their heart's real desire, even when they cloaked it with a form of religion.

A Second Chance

The universalist, however, has developed an alternative thesis, the doctrine that after death those who die in unbelief and who enter into the hell of which our Savior spoke, will be given what might be called a second chance. God will further strive with them by his Spirit of grace. And success in this further striving is a certainty. God will go on summoning men and women to repentance and faith until they give in and submit to the lordship of Jesus. Then they will move out of hell into heaven's glory.

So this is not a doctrine that denies the reality of hell. Hell is a reality, universalists say, and people do go into it. But it is only temporary; people come out of it too. In the words of Emil Brunner, in this view hell is "a pedagogic cleansing process." Hell, according to these theorists, seems to correspond to Catholic purgatory. Hell is not the ultimate but the penultimate state, and theirs is a doctrine of salvation out of what the New Testament describes as eternal punishment and eternal destruction. Scholars speak of it rightly as an optimism of grace.

What arguments could possibly be put forward to establish a view like this? Two kinds of positive arguments are used. Those in the first group are exegetical arguments; those in the second group are theological.

The exegetical arguments. Appeal is made to three classes of biblical texts. First, there are passages that seem to predict the actual salvation of all, such as "to restore everything" (Acts 3:21); I "will draw all men to myself" (Jn 12:32); through the obedience and righteousness of one man, justification and life will come to all (Rom 5:18-19); all things, even death, are going to be made subject to Christ (1 Cor 15:25-28); and "at the name of Jesus every knee should bow" (Phil 2:9-11).

There are also texts that seem to say that it is God's intention to save all: "Our Savior . . . wants all men to be saved" (1 Tim 2:3-4); "The Lord is . . . not wanting anyone to perish, but everyone to come to repentance" (2 Pet 3:9).

Finally, some Scriptures seem to tell us that the cross has brought about a relation between God and humanity that must mean universal salvation: "God was reconciling the world to himself in Christ" (2 Cor 5:19); "He . . . did not spare his own Son, but gave him up for us all" (Rom 8:32); "He is the atoning sacrifice for our sins, and not only for ours but also for the sins of the whole world" (1 Jn 2:2); Jesus tasted "death for everyone" (Heb 2:9); "the grace of God that brings salvation has appeared to all men" (Tit 2:11).

However, these three classes of texts, alleged to prove universalism, are not conclusive for several reasons. For one thing, they all admit of another explanation that is more germane to their context than the universalist one. The references to "all" and "everyone" prove in each instance to be limited by their context to those many whom God has planned to save; the "us" for whom Christ is said to have died prove to be those who now believe; the generalized references to "the world" prove on inspection to bear a sense that is moral (humans everywhere in their badness) rather than statistical (every single human being who ever was, is or will be).

Further, they are all juxtaposed with other texts that affirm that some do perish. For example, after Acts 3:21, where Peter speaks of the restoring of all things, he also says that whoever "does not listen to him [Christ] will be completely cut off from among his people" (Acts 3:23). The Lord who in John 12:32 is found saying, "I, when I am lifted up from the earth, will draw all men to myself," had previously said that some would be raised from the dead for the resurrection of condemnation (Jn 5:29). And while in Philippians 2:10 Paul says that "at the name of Jesus every knee should bow," he says in the next chapter (3:19) that the end of some people is destruction.

Finally, there is no Scripture for any pleading of God with men and women after death. Universalists have appealed to 1 Peter 3:18-20, which says that Christ "went and preached to the spirits in prison who disobeyed long ago when God waited patiently in the days of Noah." But however you expound that text, it certainly does not provide a basis for asserting that there will now be preaching by our Lord after death to every soul in hell, let alone that such preaching will be successful in every case.

There is no ground for challenging the old doctrine of eternal punishment on exegetical lines. With that verdict modern universalists for the most part agree. So they move from exegetical to theological arguments.

The theological arguments. These are based principally on two considerations: the character of God, and the victory of the cross.

The New Testament declares that God is love. It is unthinkable, universalists say, that he should have any other intention than to save all his rational creatures from the sin into which they have fallen. His love in redemption must be as wide as his love in creation, and because he is sovereign and omnipotent, this purpose cannot fail. "God has no permanent problem children" (Nels Ferre). The late John Robinson, in his book *In the End, God,* says that the justice of God must be thought of as a function of his love. But surely it is enough to reply that in the Bible the attributes of God are never represented as being attributes of each other, and certainly not in this case.

The Scripture tells us that God is holy and that within his holiness redeeming love is manifested in the salvation of believers, while retributive justice is manifested in the condemnation of unbelievers. John, who says that God is love (1 Jn 4:8), had earlier affirmed that God is light (1 Jn 1:5). The universalists say that to have any of his creatures suffering eternally would be hell to God. But where does the Bible tell us anything like that? This is a speculation that has no links with the biblical witness to the mystery of the divine being.

A second theological argument that some universalists use derives directly from their belief concerning the victory of the cross. The cross, it is said, actually secured the salvation of all, and therefore our faith or lack of it is not objectively decisive. Faith is simply a matter of coming to recognize that you have already been saved; then you smile, as it were, and say to God, "Thank you very much!" This conception, however, parts company with Scripture.

The New Testament says that salvation is found only in Christ. None are in Christ till they have been brought into Christ, and men and women are not brought into Christ without faith. Faith is essential. Reconciliation must be received, and those who do not receive it are without it. "Whoever believes in him is not condemned, but whoever does not believe stands condemned already. . . . God's wrath remains on him" (Jn 3:18, 36). "The gospel . . . is the power of God for the salvation of everyone who believes" (Rom 1:16). The Scripture seems to make it clear that the victory of Calvary brings salvation to no one until he or she puts personal trust in Jesus Christ.

In addition, the New Testament defines the saving purpose and effect of the cross in particularistic terms. "Christ loved the church and gave himself up for her" (Eph 5:25). Universalists cannot explain what this particularist limitation is doing in Scripture.

Leaving aside the special problem of those who never heard and focusing attention entirely on those who have heard the gospel, let me now ask two final questions.

Does the idea of a second probation, a probation that will issue in final success, take into account the fixity of an unregenerate person, a natural person, in bondage to sin? Wrote the late Nels Ferre, "In the afterlife God will put the screw on hard enough to make men want to change their ways." Really? Surely what both Scripture and experience suggest is that such treatment would simply produce greater hardening and further bitterness and defiance. God has no richer revelation of grace to show to Judas in the world to come than Jesus showed to Judas in the course of his life in this world; how are we to imagine God putting the screw on Judas? If people reject the gospel of Christ in this life, because sin has blinded their mind, there is no ground for expecting them to behave any differently in the world to come. Mere "moral suasion," however intense, will not change human hearts, either here or hereafter.

Further, does the idea of a successful second probation for those who die in unbelief take into account the Bible's insistence on the decisiveness of this life? There was a great gulf fixed between Dives and Lazarus (Lk 16:26). And "man is destined to die once, and after that to face judgment" (Heb 9:27). There is no suggestion of any successful second probation in these verses. The letter to the Hebrews tells us it is a fearful thing to fall into the hands of the living God. "We must all appear before the judgment seat of Christ, that each one may receive what is due him for the things done while in the body" (2 Cor 5:10). The actual things done in the body will come back to us as our destiny, a destiny that we made for ourselves by our choices here and that God in his last solemn act of respect for the reality of human responsibility will duly award us.

God will ask, "Have you chosen to be without me? Then you will be without me!" Did you choose in this world to live your life apart from Jesus? Jesus in that world will say, "Depart from me. You will have the separation you have chosen." That, as we have seen, is the essence of the biblical doctrine of judgment and hell. Eternal destinies are made in this life. "Now is the time of God's favor, now is the day of salvation" (2 Cor 6:2). It seems necessary, therefore, to dismiss universalist speculations, however attractive, as unfounded and untrue.

A century ago James Denney wrote, "I dare not say to myself that if I forfeit the opportunity this life affords I shall ever have another; and therefore I dare not say so to another man." To offer others a hope that you would not dare embrace for yourself is not charity but cynicism. Surely for thoughtful and responsible people Denney's comment is in every sense the last word on this subject.

13

CHRISTIANITY & WORLD RELIGIONS

C HRISTIANITY HAS ALWAYS BEEN A MISSIONARY RELIGION. At the close of his earthly ministry our Lord commissioned his followers to go and make disciples of all nations (Mt 28:19). It is generally recognized today that the church has no right to call itself apostolic unless it acknowledges this missionary obligation. The universal missionary imperative implies an exclusive claim, a claim made by our Lord himself: "I am the way and the truth and the life. No one comes to the Father except through me" (Jn 14:6).

Only One Saving Religion

To deny that any can know the Father apart from Christ is to affirm that non-Christian religion is powerless to bring them to God and effective only to keep them from him. Accordingly, the summons to put faith in Christ must involve a demand for the endorsement of this adverse verdict and for the avowed renunciation of non-Christian faith as empty and, indeed, demonic falsehood. "Turn from these worthless things to the living God" (Acts 14:15)—that was what the gospel meant for those who worshiped the Greek pantheon at Lystra in Paul's day, and that is what it means for the adherents of non-Christian religions now. The gospel calls their worship idolatry (1 Thess 1:9) and their deities demons (1 Cor 10:20), and asks them to accept this evaluation as part of their repentance and faith.

This point must be constantly and obtrusively made, for to play down the impotence of non-Christian religion would obscure the glory of Christ as the *only* Savior. "There is no other name under heaven given to men by which we must be saved" (Acts 4:12). If Christless religion can save, the incarnation and atonement were superfluous. Only, therefore, as the church insists that Christless religion, of whatever shape or form and however impressive in its own way, is bankrupt so far as salvation is concerned can it avoid seeming to countenance the suspicion that for some people, at any rate, our Lord's death was really needless.

It is beyond dispute that this is the biblical position, but naturally it raises questions. How does the gospel evaluate the religions that it seeks to displace? How, in view of its condemnation of them, does it account for the moral and intellectual achievements of their piety and theology? And how does it propose to set about commending Christ to their sincere and convinced adherents without giving an impression of ignorance, intolerance, patronage or conceit?

These questions press more acutely today than at any time since the Reformation, and there are three reasons for this. In the first place, this century's intensive study of comparative religion has made available more knowledge than the church ever had before about the non-Christian faiths of the world, and in particular about the intellectual and mystical strength of the highest forms of Eastern religion. This makes it necessary at least to qualify the sweeping dismissal of these faiths as ugly superstitions that to earlier missionary thinkers, who knew only the seamy side of Eastern popular piety, seemed almost axiomatic. Fair dealing is a Christian duty, and every body of opinion has a right to be assessed by its best representatives as well as its worst. (How would historic Christianity fare if measured solely by popular piety down the ages?)

In the second place, the great Asian faiths, Hinduism, Buddhism and especially Islam, are reviving and gaining ground partly, no doubt, through the impetus given them by the ever-growing fascination with them in the West. It is no longer possible naively to assume, as our evangelical grandfathers often did, that these religions must soon wither and die as the gospel advances. As we meet them today, they are not moribund but confident, aggressive and forward-looking, critical of Christian ideas and convinced of their own superiority. How are we to speak to their present condition?

In the third place, Christian evangelism has been accused and to some extent convicted by Eastern people of having in the past formed part of a larger cultural, and sometimes imperialistic, program of Westernization. These thinkers now tend to dismiss Christianity as a distinctively Western faith and its exclusive claim as one more case of Western cultural arrogance. They insist that the present aspirations of the East are compatible only with indigenous Eastern forms of religion.

There seems no doubt that Protestant missionary policy during the last hundred years has invited this tragic misunderstanding. Too often it proceeded on the unquestioned assumption that to export the outward forms of Western civilization was part of the missionary's task, and that indigenous churches should be given no more than colonial status in relation to the mother church from which the missionaries had come. It is not surprising that such a policy has been both misunderstood and resented.

The Protestant missionary enterprise needs urgently to learn to explain itself to the new nations in a way that makes clear it is not part of a cunning plan for exporting the American or British way of life but is something quite different. This necessitates a reappraisal on our part of non-Christian religions that will be, if not less critical in conclusions, more sympathetic, respectful and theologically discriminating in method than was the case in earlier days. Christian missionary enterprise inevitably gives offense to those of other faiths simply by existing, but the church must watch to see that the offense given is always that of the cross and never that of cultural snobbery and imperialism on the part of the missionaries.

It seems that the need for a deepening of accuracy and respect in the evangelistic dialogue with other religions is more pressing than evangelical Christians generally realize. This, perhaps, is because evangelical missionary effort during the past century has been channeled largely through fairly small inter- or nondenominational societies that have concentrated on pioneer and village work, whereas it is in the towns that resentment and suspicion of the missionary movement are strongest. But it is very desirable that evangelicals should appreciate the situation and labor to give the necessary lead. They are uniquely qualified to do this, having been preserved from the confusion about the relation of Christianity to other religions that has clouded the greater part of Protestant thinking since the heyday of liberalism eighty years ago. Though liberalism is now generally disavowed, its ideas still have influence. And its ideas on this particular subject are the reverse of helpful, as we will now see.

Liberal Bias Lingers

The liberal philosophy (you could not call it a theology) of religion was built on two connected principles, both of which have a pedigree going back to the philosophical idealism of Hegel and the religious romanticism of Schleiermacher. The first principle was that the essence of religion is the same everywhere, that religion is a genus wherein each particular religion is a more or less highly developed species. This idea was usually linked with the reading of the human race's religious history as a record of ascent from animistic magical rites through ritualistic polytheism to the heights of ethical monotheism—a speculative schematization, the evolutionary shape of which gave it a vogue much greater than the evidence for it warrants. (In fact, the evidence for primitive monotheism and for recurring degeneration from noble beginnings as the real pattern of humankind's religious history seems a good deal stronger. Romans 1:18-32 cannot now be dismissed as historically groundless fantasy.)

The second principle, following from the first, was that creeds and dogmas are no more than the byproducts of moral and mystical experience—attempts, that is, to express religious intuitions verbally in order to induce similar experiences in others. Theological differences, in this view, can have no ultimate significance. All religion grows out of an intuition, more or less pure and deep, of the same infinite. All religions are climbing the same mountain to the seat of the same transcendent being. The most that can be said of their differences is that they are going up by different routes, some of which appear less direct and may not reach quite to the top.

If these ideas are accepted, the only question that can be asked when two religions meet is, Which of these is the higher and more perfect specimen of its kind? And this question is to be answered by comparing not their doctrines but their piety and the characteristic religious experiences that their piety enshrines. For religions are not the sort of things that are true or false, nor are their doctrines more than their byproducts. Nor, indeed, has any existing form of religion more than a relative validity; the best religion yet may still be superseded by a worthier one. Accordingly, the only possible justification for Christian missions is that Christians, whose piety and ethics may represent the highest in religion that has emerged to date, are bound by the rule of charity to share their possessions with people of other faiths—not in order to displace those faiths but to enrich them and to be enriched by them. Then, it is surmised, from this pooling of religious experience a still higher form of religion may well be developed. This position was expounded at the academic level by Troeltsch and on the popular level in documents such as the American laymen's inquiry *Rethinking Missions* (1931), which the late Hendrik Kraemer described as "devoid of real theological sense . . . a total distortion of the Christian message," involving "a suicide of missions and an annulment of the Christian faith." Many of today's New Agers hold views of this kind, and the Parliament of Religions in Chicago in 1993 gave these ideas a thorough airing.

A Change for the Better
Since the middle of this century, however, the theological atmosphere has changed overall for the better. The liberal philosophy of religions has been demolished by the broadsides of such writers as Barth, Brunner and Kraemer himself, and attention is being given once again to the theology of religions found in the Bible.

What is this theology? It can be summed up in the following formula: Christianity is a religion of revelation received; all other faiths are religions of revelation denied. This we must briefly explain.

Christianity is a religion of revelation received. It is a religion of faith in a special revelation, given through specific historical events, of salvation for sinners. The object of Christian faith, as we have seen already, is the Creator's disclosure of himself as the triune Savior of his guilty creatures through the mediation of Jesus Christ, the Father's Word and Son. This is a disclosure authoritatively reported and interpreted in the God-inspired pages of Holy Scripture. Faith is trust in the Christ of history who is the Christ of the Bible. The revelation that the gospel declares and faith receives is God's gracious answer to the question of human sin. Its purpose is to restore guilty rebels to fellowship with their Maker. Faith in Christ is no less God's gift than is the Christ of faith; the faith that receives Christ is created in fallen human beings by the sovereign work of the Spirit, restoring spiritual sight to our blind minds. Thus true Christian faith is an adoring acknowledgment of the omnipotent mercy of God both in providing a perfect Savior for hopeless, helpless sinners and in drawing them to him.

Non-Christian religions are religions of revelation denied. They are religions that spring from the suppression and distortion of a general revelation concerning the being and law of the Creator, a revelation that is given in and through humankind's knowledge of God's world. The primary word on this comes from Romans 1:18-32 and 2:12-15. Paul there tells us that the "invisible qualities" of God—his deity and creative power—are not merely discernible but actually discerned by humankind ("God has made it plain" to them; these qualities are "clearly seen," 1:19-20). This discernment brings knowledge of the obligation of worship and thanksgiving (vv. 20-21), the duties of the moral law (2:14-15), God's wrath against ungodliness (1:18), and death as the penalty of sin (1:32). General revelation is adapted only to the needs of human beings in innocence and answers only the question, What does God require of his rational creatures? It speaks of wrath against sin but not of mercy for sinners. Hence it can bring nothing but disquiet to fallen persons. But humankind prefers not to face it, labors to falsify it and willfully perverts its truth into the lie of idolatry (1:25) by habitual lawlessness (1:18). Human creatures are worshiping beings who have refused in their pride to worship their Maker, so they turn the light of divine revelation into the darkness of human-made religion and enslave themselves to unworthy deities of their own devising, made in their own image or that of creatures inferior to themselves (1:23). This is the biblical explanation of nonbiblical religion, from the crudest to the most refined.

Flashes of Common Grace

Yet God in common grace prevents the truth from being utterly suppressed. Flashes of light break through that we should watch for and gratefully recognize, as did Paul at Athens when he quoted Aratus (Acts 17:28). And no part of general revelation is universally obscured. Despite all attempts to smother them, these truths keep seeping through the back of our mind, creating uneasiness and prompting fresh efforts to blanket the obtrusive light. Hence we may expect to find in all non-Christian religions certain recurring characteristic tensions that never really get resolved. These are a restless sense of the hostility of the powers of the universe; an undefined feeling of guilt and all sorts of merit-making techniques designed to get rid of it; a dread of death and a consuming anxiety to feel that one has conquered it; forms of worship aimed at once to placate, bribe and control the gods, and to make them keep their distance except when wanted; an alarming readiness to call moral evil good, and good evil, in the name of religion; and an ambivalent attitude of mind that seems both to seek God and to seek to evade him in the same act.

Judaism and Islam are at this point special cases, since, while denying Christ, they both build in their own way on the special revelation of the Old Testament. Both negate the plurality of persons in the Godhead, so they cannot embrace the gospel of Father, Son and Spirit working together for the sinner's salvation. Both negate the incarnation, the atonement and the new birth, so neither knows the reality of fellowship with Jesus and the life of grateful love to God that together are the hallmark of Christianity. Though intellectually closer to Christianity than some other religions are, they need the light of the gospel of Christ and the purging of mistaken ideas no less than other religions do.

Therefore, in our evangelistic dialogue with non-Christian faiths, our task must be to present the biblical revelation of God in Christ not as supplementing them but as explaining their existence, exposing their errors and judging their inadequacy. We will measure them consistently by what they say or omit to say about God and our relation to him. We will labor to show the real problem of religion to which the gospel gives the answer, namely, how a sinner may get right with his or her Maker. We will diligently look for the hints and fragments of truth these religions contain and appeal to them (set in their proper theological perspective) as pointers to the true knowledge of God. And finally, we will do all this under a sense of compulsion (for Christ has sent us), in love (for non-Christians are our fellow creatures and without Christ they cannot be saved) and with all humility (for we are sinners ourselves, and there is nothing, no part of our message, not even our faith, that we have not received as a gift). So with help from on high, we will continue to honor God and serve humankind by evangelistic witness in the world of religions, affirming still that faith in our Lord and Savior Jesus Christ is the greatest and most universal of all human needs.

14

THE REALITY
OF HELL

T O ANY NORMAL PERSON, THE THOUGHT THAT PEOPLE ONE knows and cares for, not to mention oneself, might face a destiny that could be described as eternal punishment will be profoundly disturbing. It rudely disrupts the sort of peace of mind that we in the Western world cultivate today—the peace of mind that is gained by constantly telling oneself that there is nothing to worry about and everything will work out all right in the end. But since this complacency is part of our culture and is sniffed like glue in the air we breathe, and does in fact operate as a deadening drug on the mind, it is a kind of knee-jerk reaction with us to resent having it disturbed. From thence comes our tendency to dismiss the doctrine of eternal punishment in all its forms as debased Christianity. We scoff at hell fire as a bad dream, the murky stamping ground of redneck fundamentalists, backwoods preachers and old-fashioned Roman Catholics, and we write off the idea as a hangover from primitive ages now long past.

So when we meet people who still believe in eternal punishment, we regard them as at least quaint and perhaps weird. We certainly do not take them seriously. We know, of course, that belief in eternal punishment has been part of the mainstream of Christian conviction from the first. Maybe we know that Tertullian in the third century and Thomas Aquinas in the thirteenth taught that the sufferings of those in hell would be a joyful spectacle to those in heaven. This notion was affirmed also by Jonathan Edwards, whose famous or infamous sermon "Sinners in the Hands of an Angry God" was, so we were taught at school, the product of a sick and morbid mind. We know too that belief in eternal punishment bulked large in all forms of Victorian Christianity. But just as we would not dream of aping the Victorians in other matters, so we acquit ourselves of any responsibility to go along with them in this. Hell is dead, we say, so back to peace of mind!

Whatever Became of Hell?

How should we respond to this? I have no particular desire to defend Victorian Christianity or Edwards or Aquinas or Tertullian. But I do most certainly desire to defend that to which they all appealed, namely, the Christianity taught by the Lord Jesus Christ and his apostles. My first task now must be to point out as forcefully as I can that, as we saw earlier, Jesus and the apostles do not let us off the hook with regard to eternal punishment as we so blithely let ourselves off it. Rather, they impale us on that hook and make us face this issue directly. The doctrine of eternal punishment stems directly from Jesus, and the apostolic teaching on the subject simply echoes what the founder of Christianity first said. And no Greek myth maker or Jewish apocalyptic fantasist ever spoke of eternal punishment with such weight and gravity as Jesus did. As W. G. T. Shedd affirmed in a landmark statement a century ago:

> The strongest support of doctrine of Endless Punishment is the teaching of Christ, the Redeemer of men. . . . Christ could not have warned so frequently and earnestly as He did against "the fire that shall never be quenched," and "the worm that dieth not," had he known that there is

no future peril to fully correspond to them. Jesus Christ is the person who is responsible for the doctrine of Eternal Perdition. He is the Being with whom all opponents of this theological tenet are in conflict.

This is a strong statement, but the evidence warrants it, as we will see.

In chapter 12 we discussed the doctrine of universalism and argued for the reality of eternal punishment on the basis of Matthew 25:46 in its context. Eternal punishment, as Jesus pictures it in this passage, is departure into "eternal fire prepared for the devil and his angels" (v. 41). Of that fire Jesus had spoken often, using for it the word *gehenna*, the Greek form of *Ge Hinnom*, "Valley of Hinnom." This was an area outside the wall of Jerusalem where children had once been offered as burnt sacrifices to Molech (2 Chron 28:3; 33:6), and which had become the city's incinerator area, where the garbage and the discarded corpses of those without families were daily burned. In the Sermon on the Mount we find Jesus saying to his own professed disciples that anyone calling his brother a fool (an index of malicious contempt in one's heart) "will be in danger of the fire of hell" (literally, "the Gehenna of fire," Mt 5:22). In Matthew 18:9 he refers again to the fire: "If your hand or your foot causes you to sin, cut it off and throw it away. It is better for you to enter life maimed or crippled than to have two hands or two feet and be thrown into eternal fire. And if your eye causes you to sin, gouge it out and throw it away. It is better for you to enter life with one eye than to have two eyes and be thrown into the fire of hell" (Mt 18:8-9).

Another version of this same bit of teaching in Mark's Gospel speaks of a person with two hands going into "hell, where the fire never goes out" and of a person with two eyes being "thrown into hell, where 'their worm does not die, and the fire is not quenched' " (Mk 9:43, 47-48, echoing imagery from Is 66:24, which speaks of the worm and the fire destroying corpses, but applying the imagery to the fate of living souls).

With all this should be linked Jesus' picture of tares and bad fish

With all this should be linked Jesus' picture of tares and bad fish being finally taken out of the kingdom and thrown into "the fiery furnace [literally, 'the furnace of the fire'], where there will be weeping and gnashing of teeth" (Mt 13:42, 50). Related to this also is the grim form of Jesus' call for courage as he sends out the Twelve on a mission: "Do not be afraid of those who kill the body but cannot kill the soul. Rather, be afraid of the One who can destroy both soul and body in hell" (Mt 10:28). "Destroy" in that verse is *apollumi,* the regular Greek word for wrecking and ruining something, so making it useless for its intended purpose, and "hell" is *gehenna.* The One to be feared is not the devil but the One whom Jesus called Father.

What does all this add up to? We may summarize as follows: Jesus speaks of a destiny of being in the fire for all those everywhere (in Matthew 25:32 the sheep and the goats are between them "all the nations") whom he does not accept as his own. He calls the fire Gehenna and describes it as part of the abiding future order of things and as never going out. To enter or be thrown into it (Jesus uses both verbs) brings unqualified distress ("weeping and gnashing of teeth"— a condition that Jesus elsewhere ascribes to those banished at the Judgment Day to the darkness outside, Matthew 8:12; 22:13; 25:30).

Clearly, we are in the world of imagery here, for the fire and the darkness are both picturing the same condition, one of painful and hopeless desolation. Equally clearly, the condition being pictured is unimaginably dreadful and worth any labor and any cost to avoid. And the speaker is the incarnate Son of God, our divine instructor, who should know what he is talking about and should therefore be heard as having authority when he deals with these things.

The apostolic writers use their own vocabulary but do no more, just as they do no less, than follow in their Master's footsteps. Here are some sample passages. In Romans 2:5-6, Paul warns each impenitent person thus: "you are storing up wrath against yourself for the day of God's wrath, when his righteous judgment will be revealed. God 'will give to each person according to what he has done' " (a quote from Ps 62:12). And further: "For those who are self-seeking and who reject the truth and follow evil, there will be wrath and anger. There will be trouble and distress for every human being who does evil. . . . God does not show favoritism. All who sin apart from the law will also perish apart from the law, and all who sin under the law will be judged by the law. . . . This will take place on the day when God will judge men's secrets through Jesus Christ, as my gospel declares" (Rom 2:8-9, 11-12, 16). Thus Paul states the principle and affirms the certainty of final judgment and final ruin.

More dramatically, Paul also declares, "When the Lord Jesus is revealed from heaven in blazing fire, . . . he will punish those who do not know God and do not obey the gospel of our Lord Jesus. They will be punished with everlasting destruction and shut out from the presence of the Lord" (2 Thess 1:7-9).

Jude's brief letter includes both of Jesus' images for the state of final loss. Verse 7 reads, "Sodom and Gomorrah and the surrounding towns gave themselves up to sexual immorality. . . . They serve as an example of those who suffer the punishment of *eternal fire*." Verse 13 speaks of certain immoral folk in the church as "wandering stars, for whom *blackest darkness* [literally, as in the KJV, 'the blackness of darkness'] has been reserved for ever" (emphasis added). It has sometimes been suggested that the eternal fire is an image of immediate annihilation, but Jude's phrase "darkness . . . reserved for ever" surely indicates that he did not mean his words about the fire to be taken that way.

In the book of Revelation the long visionary appendix to the Lord's letters (chs. 4—22) intensifies the Lord's picture of eternal fire in a deliberately excruciating way, doing canonically what "Sinners in the Hands of an Angry God" attempted later, and for the same reason: to lead people to embrace and hold fast life in Christ and not to risk the alternative. Revelation 14:9-11 warns that anyone who worships the beast "will be tormented with burning sulfur in the presence of the holy angels and of the Lamb. And the smoke of their torment rises for ever and ever." Revelation 20:10 pictures a lake of burning sulfur into which at the Last Judgment the devil, the beast and the false prophet are thrown, to be "tormented day and night for ever and ever." Then in verse 14 death and Hades are thrown into the lake, and it is identified with "the second death," which verse 6 had told us would have no power over God's saints. After that, climactically, verse 15 declares, "If anyone's name was not found written in the book of life, he was thrown into the lake of fire." In the context of this and in light of the explicit statement of 14:11, it is unnatural to suppose, as some do, that being thrown into the lake of fire means anything less than pain and grief without end.

It is true that in the intertestamental literature of Judaism (such books as 2 and 4 Maccabees, the Wisdom of Solomon, Judith, Ecclesiasticus, Jubilees, 2 Baruch, and the Assumption of Moses) the imagery of Gehenna and predictions of unending future torment for the ungodly are already present. Jesus and the apostles were therefore drawing on a stock of ideas and beliefs that already existed. This does not, however, in any way lessen the divine authority of these notions when the New Testament teachers endorse them. Moreover, *endorse* is hardly the right word, for in using these ideas Jesus and the apostles purged them of the overtones of gloating that they had often carried before and imparted to them a nuance or tone of what I can only call traumatic awe: a passionate gladness that justice will be done for God's glory, linked with an equally passionate sadness that fellow human beings, no matter how perverse, will thereby be ruined. This traumatic awe is reflected in Jesus' tearful words on Jerusalem (Lk 19:41-44) and in his compassionate admonition to the women walking with him to Calvary ("Daughters of Jerusalem, do not weep for me; weep for yourselves and for your children," Lk 23:28). Similar submissive sadness comes out in Paul's heart cry about the Jews whose rejection by God he announces: "I have great sorrow and unceasing anguish in my heart. For I could wish that I myself were cursed and cut off from Christ for the sake of my brothers. . . . My heart's desire and prayer to God for the Israelites is that they may be saved" (Rom 9:2-3; 10:1).

The same traumatic awe will strike the soul of every thoughtful Christian with unconverted relatives and friends who takes seriously the promise that Jesus the Savior will one day return to judge the living and the dead. And surely we may boldly say that though it is not in the least comfortable, yet it is healthy for us to feel this trauma. Like Paul before us, we find relief from the pain only in wholehearted commitment to the ministry of spreading the gospel, in which we become all things to all people so that we may save some (1 Cor 9:22). And we seek to fulfill Jude's blunt summons: "Snatch others from the fire and save them" (Jude 23). The only spiritual method of alleviating distress at the prospect of souls being lost is to take action to win them. God enables us to live with the prospect of people we know possibly being lost, by moving us to pray and work so that they may not be lost, and indeed by using that prospect in our consciences to stir us up to witness to them in an evangelistic way.

The Language of Punishment

But the eternal punishment of all the ungodly nonetheless remains a distressing truth to discuss. This makes it vital to have for the purpose words that are conceptually clear but not emotionally loaded. I prefer to speak of retribution rather than punishment, that is (saying it more precisely), the *divinely executed retributive process that operates in the world to come.* Let me explain why I choose this form of words.

First, though the language of punishment, in the sense of God's judicial infliction, is abundantly scriptural, it conjures up unhelpful suspicions. The dictum of Goethe "We should always distrust anyone who has a desire to punish" would nowadays be reinforced by the followers of Freud. Modern thought is skeptical as to whether punishment that does not serve the purpose of reforming the offender and safeguarding others can ever be justified. Talk about God's punitive role on the last day, when neither of these further goals can enter into the reckoning, is bound to feed the suspicion that God is in truth arbitrary and vindictive in a way that is not quite admirable, because it is not quite moral. Indeed, the widespread revolt against the idea of eternal punishment during the past century has sprung from this suspicion and from a desire for a doctrine that does not thus impugn God's character. So I think it best not to use the vocabulary of punishment at all.

Second, though admittedly clumsy the phraseology of retribution is not emotionally loaded, and it should not cloud discussion by evoking prejudicial attitudes, for in our culture retribution retains its status as a moral rather than an immoral idea.

Third, individual retribution, as one aspect of the larger reality of divine judgment whereby evil is stopped in its tracks and righteousness restored, is precisely what we are talking about. The word fits. Punishment can be arbitrary and not proportionate to the wrongdoing, but retribution means that one's past becomes the decisive factor in determining one's present, for one gets what one deserves.

And then, last, the language of retribution permits in a way that punishment language does not, the blending in our minds of two thoughts that are blended in the Bible. These are the thought of condemnation justly imposed by God as the Judge, vindicating righteousness, and the thought that this is self-inflicted through our own perversity in choosing death rather than life. This biblical blending is clearest in John 3:18-20, where, having stated that "whoever does not believe stands condemned already because he has not believed in the name of God's one and only Son," John continues: "This is the process [so Leon Morris renders *krisis,* the Greek word used here]: Light has come into the world, but men loved darkness instead of light. . . .

Everyone who does evil . . . will not come into the light for fear that his deeds will be exposed." In other words, we choose to retreat from God rather than repent before God, and God's judicial sentence is a ratifying for eternity of the sentence of separation from God that we by our own choice have already passed on ourselves. Teachers like C. S. Lewis stress the thought that no one is in hell who has not chosen to be there, in the sense of choosing to be self-absorbed and to keep God out of his or her life, and that is evidently one aspect of the grim truth. It is an aspect that the idea of retribution readily covers.

It may be that someone is wondering why I choose to write on this somber theme. I do so because in today's Christianity what I am now calling the divinely executed retributive process that operates in the world to come is becoming more and more a problem area for belief. Uncertainty is growing, and growing in a way that has a weakening effect on Christian witness. Hence the inclusion here of a theology of hell. It is an essential part of the faith.

One final admonition, however. Do not speculate about the retributive process. Do not try to imagine what it is like to be in hell. The horrific imaginings of the past were hardly helpful and often in fact proved a stumbling block, as people equated the reality of hell with the lurid word pictures drawn by Dante or Edwards or C. H. Spurgeon. Not that these men were wrong to draw their pictures, any more than Jesus was wrong to dwell on the fire and the worm. The mistake is to take such pictures as physical descriptions, when in fact they are imagery symbolizing realities of which we can only say that they are far, far more dreadful than the symbols themselves. The words used by theologians, on the basis of Scripture, to describe hell—loss of all good, all pleasure, all rest and all hope; exclusion from God's favor and exposure to his anger; remorse, frustration, fury, despair; self-hate as a form of self-absorption; introversion to the point of idiocy—are formal categories only. What they might mean in actual experience for anyone is more than we can imagine, and we are wise not to try.

Our wisdom is rather to spend our lives finding ways of showing gratitude for the saving grace of Christ that ensures that we will never in fact go to the hell that each of us so richly deserves. We should school our minds to dwell on heaven rather than on the other place, except when we are seeking, in Jude's phrase, to snatch others from the fire (Jude 23), as the Lord Jesus did before us. The Puritans, who are so often credited with an obsessional interest in hell were in fact heavenly minded in just this fashion, and we will do well to follow their good example.

15

His Ascension, Our Future Hope

THE PRESENTATION OF CHRIST TODAY BY CHRISTIAN PREACH-ers and teachers tends to move straight from the historical fact of the resurrection to the contemporary encounter with the risen Lord. This sequence of themes is meant partly to challenge skeptics who deny miracles and partly to engage liberals, formalists, moralists, Jews, New Agers and adherents of other religions for whom the Jesus of history is a great teacher and a wonderful example but not a living Savior. Let us by all means go on telling people that Jesus' resurrection is one of the best-attested facts of history, for indeed it is. Let us also continue to tell them that Jesus is alive, well, accessible and present with every believer as guide and counselor, master and friend, for that is true too. But let us not lose sight of the fact that the resurrection was the prelude to the ascension. We should never forget that from the moment Jesus left the tomb, he was heading for the heavenly throne. The forty days on earth should be seen as a stopover en route.

Resurrection and Ascension

The Apostles' Creed ties Christ's resurrection directly to his ascension and heavenly reign. "The third day he rose again from the dead; he ascended into heaven and sits on the right hand of God the Father Almighty." The resurrection began and the ascension completed his return to the glory he knew before.

Jesus' first conversation after being raised from death showed this clearly. Mary of Magdala, meeting him alive again, wanted to embrace him. Matthew 28:9 says that she and the other Mary did what one did in those days to show affection to a superior: they got down and grasped his feet. But Jesus said to them, "Stop clinging to Me, for I have not yet ascended to the Father; but go to My brethren, and say to them, 'I ascend to My Father and your Father, and My God and your God' " (Jn 20:17, NASB). Jesus' words were not a cold-hearted brushoff but a compassionate reeducation. The Marys, and the rest of his disciples with them, had to get used to practicing fellowship with a Savior whom they could not touch or even see, for he would shortly ascend to heaven and so withdraw from human sight till his second coming.

Incarnation and Mystery

The resurrection and ascension involve mystery—basically, the mystery of incarnation itself. What immediate changes in the human body of the Son of God did his resurrection bring? Continuity was evident: the risen Lord looked and sounded the same as before; he was solid flesh and bone, ate food (Lk 24:39-43), and could be touched and held (Mt 28:9; Jn 20:27). But change was evident too: he could vanish and appear as it were from nowhere, even passing through locked doors (Lk 24:31, 36; Jn 20:19, 26). Some guess that Jesus' body became immaterial and invisible at the moment of the resurrection but rematerialized in some way for each of his postresurrection encounters. That certainly goes beyond the biblical evidence and arguably raises more problems than it removes. It is soberer and probably sounder to think of the resurrection as the reanimating, with enhanced powers, of a visible, material, physical organism that was destined for further transformation when the Savior, whose body it was, ascended to his Father's throne.

What exactly happened to Jesus in the ascension? The disciples' perception of this was that after he commissioned and blessed them (Lk 24:50; Acts 1:8), a cloud came down (a sign of the Father being present to act, as at the transfiguration, Luke 9:34-36), and Jesus went up—up into the cloud, leaving them staring skyward (Acts 1:9-10). That upward movement signified not only that the Father was withdrawing the Son from this world order and taking him home but also that he was advancing the Son to new dignity (as when we speak of someone's "going up in the world"). So Christ's ascension implies Christ's ascendancy; it is as if, having traveled successfully in the firm's interest, the Son was now recalled to headquarters to become managing director.

Thus the risen Lamb returned to glory to be enthroned at the Father's right hand, in the Grand Vizier position at the ancient Persian court, the place of executive government in the monarch's name. And there he reigns today, as Lord of the entire universe. As Jesus said himself, the Father has committed all authority in heaven and on earth into his hand (Mt 28:18; Jn 5:20-23, 26-27). And "he must reign until he has put all his enemies under his feet" (1 Cor 15:25).

But what should we make of Jesus' bodily exit in the cloud? It was certainly miraculous, involving a unique exercise of divine power, just as his entry into the world by virgin birth had done, but what sort of miracle was it? We should not think of Jesus as the first space traveler, zooming instantaneously through light years of distance away from us. We should find our clue, rather, in the realization that after his resurrection the three dimensions of space that confine us confined him no more. C. S. Lewis spoke of the Son being withdrawn through a "fold" in space, like an actor who, having taken his bow, appears to vanish into a fold in the stage curtain (actually, of course, stepping into the gap between the two curtains). This image gives us perhaps the best idea we can form of the mystery involved here.

The fact to be grasped is that though Jesus' *personal* presence is now available through the Holy Spirit to all who call on him everywhere, his *bodily* presence is gone. Physically, Jesus has returned to heaven, there to serve as his Father's right-hand man (how apt that phrase!) until he reappears to bring judgment.

No doubt Jesus' body in heaven is now "glorious" (Phil 3:21), shining as it did at the transfiguration. Something more has happened to it through the ascension, though we will have to wait till we ourselves get to heaven to find out just what.

Reign and Intercession

The key to understanding Jesus' present life in heaven, and with it his precious life on earth, is to grasp that he is there, as once he was here, to intercede for us. *Us* in this phrase, as always in the New Testament, means not the human race as such but past, present and future believers, all whom God has chosen to save. He intercedes in our interest in a way that guarantees our welfare by ensuring that what he died to secure for us actually becomes ours. The Son does not supplicate the Father on our behalf in uncertainty as to whether his requests will be granted. He speaks to the Father from the throne on which the Father has set him, fully aware that his will for our good is the Father's will also. Jesus' ongoing intercession for his people is therefore sovereignly efficacious.

What benefits does his intercession bring us? Quite simply, every benefit that relates to our relationship with our triune God, from every standpoint, at every level. On the one hand, Jesus' intercession maintains our justified status (Rom 8:34). On the other hand, Jesus' intercession ensures that when we approach his throne in our weakness and inadequacy, we find it to be a "throne of grace" where we "receive mercy and find grace to help us in our time of need" (Heb 4:16). No spiritual benefit of any kind comes to any child of God apart from the mediatorial intercession of Jesus the Lord.

Because Jesus has ascended to heaven, we can be sure that we too have a hope of heaven. On this Jesus was explicit and the whole New Testament is emphatic. "Father," prayed Jesus, "I want those you have given me to be with me where I am, and to see my glory" (Jn 17:24). "We shall be like him, for we shall see him as he is," declares John (1 Jn 3:2). For Christians the life to come will be the fullest enjoyment of the covenant-care relationship proclaimed in the precious words "The LORD is my shepherd" (Ps 23:1), for "the Lamb at the center of the throne will be their shepherd; he will lead them to springs of living water. And God will wipe away every tear from their eyes" (Rev 7:17). This hope, which brings joy at all times and in all circumstances, allows us to approach our own mortality with a forthright boldness that is unique to Christian believers and stands in stark contrast to the common attitude in Western society.

Facing Death

In today's world death is the great unmentionable, just as sex was a hundred years ago. Apart from cynical paradings of a sense of life's triviality (the Grateful Dead: "he who dies with the most toys wins") and egoistic expressions of belief in reincarnation (the New Age), death is not ordinarily spoken of outside of medical circles. To invite discussion of it is felt to be bad form. It has become conventional to think as if we are all going to live in this world forever and to view every case of bereavement as a reason for doubting the goodness of God. We must all know, deep down, that this is ridiculous, but we do it all the same. And in doing it we part company with the Bible and with a basic principle of right living, namely, that only when you know how to die can you know how to live. To recover Christian consistency here is an urgent need.

There is a great contrast here between past and present. In every century until our own, Christians saw this life as preparation for eternity. Medievals, Puritans and, later, evangelicals thought and wrote much about the art of dying well, and urged that our way of life should in truth be a preparation for leaving this world behind. That was not gratuitous morbidity but realistic wisdom, since death really is the one certain fact of life. Acting the ostrich with regard to it is folly to the highest degree.

Why has modern society and even modern orthodoxy so largely lost its grip on this biblical otherworldliness? Several factors have combined to produce the effect. First, death is no longer our constant companion. Until this century most children died before they were ten, and adults died at home with the family around them. But nowadays deaths in the family are rarer and, as often as not, people die out of our sight in hospitals, so that we can easily forget the certainty of our own death for years together.

Second, modern materialism, with its corollary that this life is the only life for enjoying anything, has infected Christian minds, producing the feeling that it is a cosmic outrage for anyone to have to leave this world before he or she has tasted all that it has to offer.

Third, Marxist mockery of the Christian hope ("pie in the sky when you die"), plus the accusation that having a hope of heaven destroys one's zeal for ending evil on earth, has given Christians a false conscience that inhibits them about being heavenly minded.

Fourth, modern Christians are rightly troubled at the cultural barrenness, social unconcern and seemingly shrunken humanity that have sometimes accompanied professed longings for heaven. They have come to suspect that such longings are always escapist and unhealthy. As a result, they feel guilty and inhibited about the longings for heaven that arise, often unbidden, in their own regenerate hearts.

Fifth, humanity's natural sense of being made for an eternal destiny, the awareness formerly expressed by the phrase "the greatness of the soul" has largely atrophied amid the hectic artificialities of Western urban life.

How Should We Then Die?

How should Christians think about death—their own death, to start with? Normal people do not look forward to dying, and there is good reason for that. We cannot expect the process to be pleasant; the prospect of going to give an account of oneself to God is awesome, and Christians know that physical death is the outward sign of that eternal separation from God that is the Creator's judgment on sin. This separation will become deeper and more painful through the milestone event of dying, unless saving grace intervenes. Unconverted people do well, therefore, to fear death: it is in truth fearsome.

But for Christians, death's sting is withdrawn. Grace has intervened, and now their death day becomes an appointment with their Savior, who will be there to take them to the rest prepared for them. Though they will be temporarily bodiless, which is not in itself good, they will be closer to Christ than ever before, "which is better by far" (Phil 1:23).

In addition, since believers do not know when Christ will come for them, readiness to leave this world at any time is vital Christian wisdom. Each day should find us like children looking forward to their holidays, who get packed up and ready to go a long time in advance.

The formula for this readiness is "Live each day as if thy last" (Thomas Ken). In other words, keep short accounts with God. I once heard Fred Mitchell, at that time director for the Overseas Missionary Fellowship, enforce this thought shortly before his own instantaneous homegoing, when the plane in which he was traveling disintegrated in midair. Mitchell lived what he taught, and his biography was justly given as its title the last message radioed by the pilot of the doomed plane—*Climbing on Track.* I hope never to forget his words.

Finally, dying well is one of the good works to which Christians are called, and Christ will enable us who serve him to die well, however gruesome the physical event itself. And dying thus, in Christ, through Christ and with Christ, will be a spiritual blossoming. As being born into God's spiritual kingdom was our second birthday, so being born through physical dying into the eternal world will be our third birthday. To say that a Christian's death is the end of physical life in this world is true, but to describe it as dying into the true life—"the Great Story . . . which goes on forever: in which every chapter is better than the one before," as C. S. Lewis put it—is a great deal truer.

Dag Hammarskjöld was thinking Christianly when he wrote that no philosophy that cannot make sense of death can make sense of life either, and no one's living will be right until these truths about death are anchored in his or her heart.

Scripture Index